14⁹⁵

5ᵒᵘ

W9-CNA-802

*Other titles by Paul A. Johnsgard*
*available from the University of Nebraska Press*

The Bird Decoy: An American Art Form
Birds of the Great Plains: Breeding Species and Their Distribution
Birds of the Rocky Mountains
Crane Music: A Natural History of American Cranes
Diving Birds of North America
Ducks, Geese, and Swans of the World
Grouse and Quails of North America
The Grouse of the World
A Guide to North American Waterfowl
The Nature of Nebraska: Ecology and Biodiversity
North American Game Birds of Upland and Shoreline
The Platte: Channels in Time
The Plovers, Sandpipers and Snipes of the World
Song of the North Wind: A Story of the Snow Goose
This Fragile Land: A Natural History of the Nebraska Sandhills
Those of the Gray Wind: The Sandhill Cranes
Waterfowl: Their Biology and Natural History

# Lewis and Clark
# on the Great Plains

## A NATURAL HISTORY

*Written and Illustrated
by Paul A. Johnsgard*

University of Nebraska Press,
Lincoln and London
With the Center for Great Plains Studies,
University of Nebraska–Lincoln

© 2003 by the Board of
Regents of the University
of Nebraska ⊗
All rights reserved
Manufactured in the
United States of America
Library of Congress Cata-
loging-in-Publication
Data
Johnsgard, Paul A.
Lewis and Clark on the
Great Plains: a natural
history / written and illus-
trated by Paul A.
Johnsgard.  p.  cm.
"A Bison original."
Includes bibliographical
references and index.
ISBN 0-8032-7618-4 (pbk.:
alk. paper)
1. Natural history—West
(U.S.)
2. Lewis and Clark Expe-
dition (1804–1806)
I. Title.
QH104.5W4J65 2003
508.78—dc21
2003042691

# Contents

# Maps

# Illustrations

# Preface

The purpose of this book is to identify and describe the Great Plains animals and plants that were encountered and described by Lewis and Clark and their Corps of Discovery two centuries ago during their famous exploratory expedition of the Louisiana Purchase territories. It also attempts to place both the organisms they discovered in an ecological framework and these two explorers in a historical context as biologists. It is intended to serve as a bicentennial tribute to this remarkable exploration of the then-unknown lands comprising the Louisiana Purchase. The bicentennial of this epic journey seems an especially appropriate time to review and marvel at the expedition's accomplishments, and to reflect on the changes in the land and its associated biota that have occurred during the subsequent two hundred years of American history.

The animals selected for inclusion in this survey represent as many as possible of the identifiable species of vertebrates that were initially described, or at least apparently discovered, by the Lewis and Clark expedition while crossing the Great Plains as well as those previously known species that were described in sufficient detail to permit identification with some degree of confidence. Special attention has been given to those animal species encountered by the Corps of Discovery that were previously unknown, or ones for which important new biological information was obtained during the expedition. However, a few distinctly western and montane-adapted animals such as the blue grouse (*Dendragapus obscurus*) and pinyon jay (*Gymnorhinus cyanocephalus*) were excluded. Both of these forest-adapted birds were encountered at the very edge of the Great Plains in western Montana. A few additional western or northern species, such as the Columbian ground squirrel, lynx, and moose, were likewise deemed to be of doubtful species identification or of questionable geographic affinities. These species have been included in the survey, but their names are set off by parentheses.

The plants chosen for inclusion in the text represent all those species collected on the Great Plains and preserved as herbarium specimens that are known to be still extant. Selecting the western limits of the Great Plains in order to decide which plant species to include was a subjective exercise, but those species whose ranges fall largely or entirely outside the coverage of the *Atlas of the Flora of the Great Plains* were excluded. These include antelope bush (*Purshia tridentata*), golden currant (*Ribes aureum*), moundscale (*Atriplex gardneri*), and common monkey-flower (*Mimulus guttatus*). The comments made in the text as to Native American ritual or medicinal uses of plants derive mostly from Gilmore (1977) and Kindscher (1992); the latter reference is especially valuable as to plant medicinal properties.

This summary of the animals and plants encountered by Lewis and Clark is organized in three parts, corresponding to three broad and roughly equal geographic regions, at least in terms of river distances traveled. Accompanying the summary are maps of the major campsites and associated dates spent by the Corps of Discovery in each of these three regions. The Corps spent much more time exploring during the upstream, outward-bound phase in 1804 and 1805 than during the return journey, and this first part of the expedition was by far the richest from a biological standpoint. Almost no new species were discovered during the return trip in 1806, and the associated campsites are not mapped.

In general, the animals and plants that the expedition encountered are described only for that phase of the expedition where they were first encountered. However, a few especially important mammals (e.g., bison, pronghorn, elk, wolf, and grizzly bear) are discussed in two or all three of the geographic regions recognized here. Names of present-day states or counties as well as current town locations have often been used to provide convenient geographic reference points for the reader. Included are drawings of all the certainly discovered or initially well-described vertebrates, as well as some representative plants, especially species of genera having special ritual or medicinal value for Native Americans, such as *Artemisia*, *Juniperus*, and *Nicotiana*. The names used in the text for Native American tribes are modern ones, although alternate names used by Lewis and Clark are typically shown parenthetically.

When this book had nearly gone to press, H. Wayne Phillips's *Plants of the Lewis and Clark Expedition* (2003) appeared. He illustrated more than 80 tallgrass and high-plains species, including some that are not included here because herbarium specimens are not known to exist.

# Acknowledgments

This publication was stimulated by plans for "The Nature of Lewis and Clark on the Great Plains," a symposium and associated art exhibition coinciding with the bicentennial celebration of the 1804–6 Lewis and Clark expedition, to be held in Lincoln, Nebraska, during the spring of 2004. The art exhibition is being sponsored primarily by the University of Nebraska's Center for Great Plains Studies, to which all royalties for this publication have been assigned. The author expresses his deepest appreciation to Reece Summers, curator of the Great Plains Art Center, who first suggested the project, to Gary Moulton, whose monumental work on the Lewis and Clark papers made it feasible, and to James Stubbendieck, director of the Center for Great Plains Studies, who strongly urged that the plants of Lewis and Clark be included in the project's coverage.

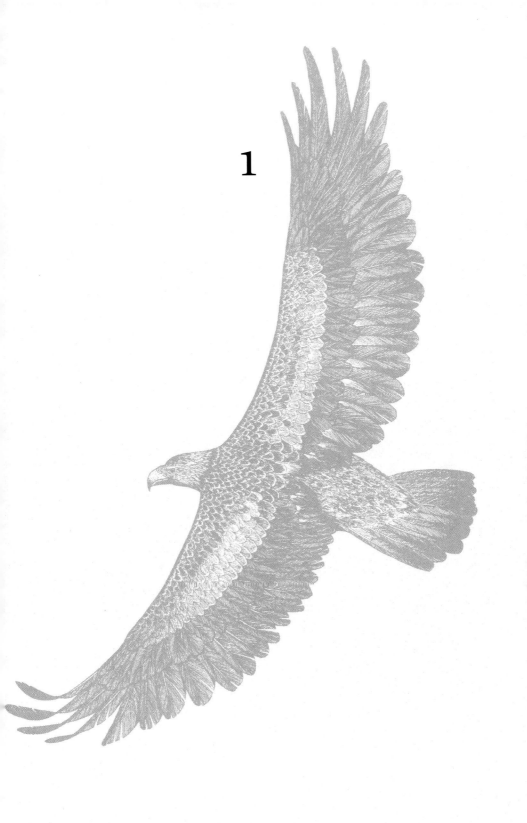

1

# Historical Overview

When Meriwether Lewis and William Clark set off up the Missouri River in mid-May of 1804 with their 26-man contingent (3 sergeants, 22 privates, and Clark's slave York) and about 10 additional boatmen and interpreters, they had no detailed knowledge of what lands or adventures lay before them. When the group returned more than two years later, in late September of 1806, they had made more discoveries of landscapes, rivers, native cultures, zoology, and botany of our continent than has any North American scientific expedition, either before or since. They traversed upstream across the entire Great Plains region, which for present purposes is defined as including that part of the Missouri Valley between the current Missouri-Kansas border and the vicinity of Three Forks, Montana, where three mountain-fed rivers merge to form the Missouri. By the time they reached what is now western Montana in late July of 1805 and were about to challenge the Rockies, they had already ascended nearly 4,000 feet of elevation. They also had explored and carefully described roughly 2,500 river miles of the Missouri Valley since leaving the Mississippi River, a task that by itself represents a heroic if not Herculean physical effort.

Over the 14-month period during which the explorers crossed the Great Plains on their way to the Pacific they collected specimens of plants later found to represent at least 20 new species, not counting an unknown number of additional specimens that either were lost or damaged beyond repair in the course of the expedition or have disappeared from any present-day museum or herbarium records.

Lewis and Clark also discovered or carefully described for the first time at least seven Great Plains species of mammals, including the pronghorn, grizzly bear, swift fox, black-tailed prairie dog, white-tailed jackrabbit, bushy-tailed woodrat, and mule deer. The Columbian ground squirrel was first encountered, and thus discovered, in western Montana, but it was not carefully described until after the group arrived in Oregon. Several Great Plains birds representing new genera (depending on the taxonomy source chosen) were described for the first time, including the greater sage-grouse, common poorwill, McCown's longspur, and Lewis's namesake species, the Lewis's woodpecker. The woodpecker, whose previously unique genus *Asyndesmus* has recently been merged with *Melanerpes*, was first seen along the edge of the Big Belt Mountains near present-day Helena, Montana. However, this woodland-edge woodpecker was not actually collected until the following spring, near Kamiah, Idaho. A skin of the Lewis's woodpecker is in Harvard University's Museum of Comparative Zoology and is perhaps the only remaining intact museum specimen of all the animals collected during the expedition. The least tern was also carefully described and measured, based on two specimens they had shot. There can be no doubt that these five species of birds, at minimum, were discovered by Lewis and Clark on the Great Plains.

In his valuable summary of the natural history of the entire expedition, Paul R. Cutright listed a total of 30 then-undescribed vertebrate species or subspecies that were noted by Lewis and Clark during the Great Plains phase and possibly as many as 9 additional ones that were encountered but not adequately described to identify them with certainty. Virginia Holmgren more recently summarized the bird discoveries of the entire expedition, listing 25 that she believed were sufficiently well described to warrant "discovery" status, 9 species that might have been considered as newly discovered if they had been better described, and 11 species that were already well known by some common name but had not yet been formally described and named scientifically. In the category of definitely discovered Great Plains birds, she listed the trumpeter swan, greater sage-grouse, semipalmated plover, mountain plover, upland sandpiper, long-billed curlew, least tern, common poorwill, Lewis's woodpecker, Sprague's pipit, McCown's longspur, western meadowlark, and Brewer's blackbird. Of these, the mountain plover and upland sandpiper are distinctly questionable as to their identification. There is no evidence that the highly elusive Sprague's pipit (*Anthus spragueii*) was ever seen, and the "small Kildee" observed along the Missouri River was probably the piping plover rather than the migratory and arctic-breeding semipalmated plover (*Charadrius semipalmatus*). The identities of several Great Plains shorebirds mentioned briefly by Lewis and Clark, such as the mountain plover and long-billed curlew, are especially problematic, as they used terms like "plover" and "curlew" rather indiscriminately for shorebirds generally. The tundra swan (*Cygnus columbianus*) (previously known as the whistling swan) was initially described from observations made by Lewis and Clark during the Pacific-slope phase of their expedition, but it or the trumpeter swan was seen earlier in what is now North Dakota. The trumpeter swan is the semiresidential breeding swan of the northern plains, whereas the arctic-breeding tundra swan is a spring and fall migrant only. Thus, the chances of their having seen the trumpeter swan on the northern plains were fairly good. At least eight previously unknown species—the trumpeter swan, greater sage-grouse, piping plover, least tern, common poorwill, Lewis's woodpecker, McCown's longspur, and western meadowlark—are well enough documented to count as having certainly been seen by Lewis and Clark, and the greater sage-grouse, least tern, and Lewis's woodpecker were as carefully described as any practicing ornithologist of the day might have done.

Among reptiles and fishes, the western rattlesnake, western hognose snake, cutthroat trout, blue catfish, channel catfish, goldeye, and mountain sucker are certain or likely to have been newly discovered species. Several Great Plains mammal and reptile species that were known but only poorly documented, such as the bison, gray wolf, coyote, western garter snake, and bullsnake, were described by Lewis and Clark to a much greater degree than previously known. Many other plains animals that later were determined to represent new subspecies of previously known species were described, or at least mentioned, for the first time.

For the trip collectively, nearly 100 previously unknown species or subspecies of vertebrate animals were encountered and variously described by Lewis and Clark, judging from a recent summary by the Sierra Club. About 40 percent of these now have a state- or federal-level designation indicating that active protection or conservation concern is warranted. Of these, 13 species are now classified as nationally endangered, including such classic Great Plains animals as the gray (prairie) wolf, whooping crane, and the interior race of the least tern. Great Plains species that were seen by the expedition members but are now federally threatened include the piping plover and grizzly bear. In the past two centuries the grizzly bear has changed from being the commonest large carnivore of the upper Missouri Valley to having been completely eradicated from it. Similar comments might be made of the gray wolf and the whooping crane.

Cutright listed a total of 22 new plant species collected by Lewis and Clark during their journey upstream between the mouth of the Kansas River and the vicinity of Three Forks, Montana. They include such plants as Indian tobacco (a species not native to the northern Great Plains), curly-top gumweed, and three species of sagebrush. A surprising number of the plants they collected were species believed by Native Americans to possess medicinal or other functional properties, and thus were very familiar to and highly valued by the tribes of the upper Missouri Valley. Most of them are now considered only to be weeds, and none is listed as threatened or endangered.

The expedition's return trip across the Great Plains in 1806 was entirely downstream and consequently much faster, thus accounting for the expedition's far fewer zoological or botanical discoveries. However, at least five Great Plains plants collected during the return trip were later described as new species, according to Cutright. These included salt sage, red false mallow, gumbo evening primrose, black greasewood, and snow-on-the-mountain. These discoveries primarily consisted of plants obtained by Captain Lewis while exploring the upper Marias River valley of northwestern Montana. Although no new plants were obtained, several new topographic features and some significant wildlife observations were documented by Captain Clark on his separate route down the Yellowstone River.

Frederick Pursh initially examined 155 of the roughly 200 plant specimens that successfully made their way back to the safety of the American Philosophical Society collections in Philadelphia. At the time he published his studies (1814), he classified four of the Lewis and Clark specimens as representing new genera and 123 as new species. A recent summary by James Reveal, Gary Moulton, and Alfred Schuyler indicate that Pursh associated the Lewis and Clark materials with 132 botanical names, 94 of which were newly proposed by him and nearly all of which were taxonomically valid. These authors also determined that Lewis and Clark collected at least 202 different kinds of plants. However, many of the Lewis and Clark specimens have since been lost. If all the plants encountered and variously described but not necessarily preserved by Lewis and Clark during their entire expedition are tallied, 176 previously unknown species or subspecies can be listed, judging from a recent summary by the Sierra Club. At least 17 new plant species were discovered while the explorers were in the Great Plains region. Gary Moulton has summarized the specimen and archival data from all the herbarium sheets currently known to exist in volume 12 of his definitive 13-volume *Journals of the Lewis and Clark Expedition*. Names of the plants mentioned here follow this reference, sometimes with parenthetical synonyms of Latin or English vernacular names that have appeared in relevant literature, such as the books of Paul Cutright and Raymond Burroughs. The plants and animal species described in the text are arranged in alphabetic sequence using English names, and both the Latin and English names are those currently recognized as official. Alternate names given in quotes, including a few place names, are those used by Lewis and Clark, and their often innovative spelling has in such cases been retained.

In the course of the expedition the group lived off the land, killing and eating almost anything they could. Burroughs compiled a list of game killed in the course of the expedition, largely for human consumption. At minimum, it included 1,001 deer, 35 elk, 227 bison, 62 pronghorns, 113 beaver, 104 geese and brant, 48 shorebirds ("plovers"), 46 grouse, 45 ducks and coots, and 9 turkeys. They also killed 43 grizzly bears, 23 black bears, 18 wolves, and 16 otters. This level of resource exploitation marked the beginning of a century of unrestrained wildlife slaughter in America, ending in the elimination of the bison, elk, gray wolf, and grizzly bear from the Great Plains, and the complete extinction of the passenger pigeon, Carolina parakeet, and Eskimo curlew.

Exactly a century after the beginning of the Lewis and Clark expedition (1903), President Theodore Roosevelt established in Florida the first of our national wildlife refuges, and the long road toward the preservation and restoration of our wildlife resources was at last under way. There are now more than 530 national wildlife refuges in the United States, of which the Charles M. Russell National Wildlife Refuge in Montana is much the largest of those situated along the Lewis and Clark route. There are 20 national grasslands, totaling 4 million acres, 17 of which are in the western Great Plains from North Dakota and Montana to New Mexico and Texas. There are now also 155 national forests, covering almost 200 million acres, including the Lewis and Clark National Forest, located between the Missouri and Yellowstone Rivers of Montana. Also, there are 300 Indian reservations, now still home to members of about 500 tribes; ten of these reservations occur along the Missouri River between Nebraska and Montana, some of them supporting direct descendants of the people first encountered by Lewis and Clark.

> I shall vanish and be no more,
> But the land over which I now roam
> Shall remain, and change not.

*Anonymous Omaha Indian*

# Kansas-Missouri and Nebraska-Iowa

## Summary of Route and Major Biological Discoveries

U ntil the Corps of Discovery reached the vicinity of present-day Kansas (the mouth of the Kansas River) in late June, they had not entered true wilderness and had made only one zoological discovery of interest—their capture on May 31, 1804, of several specimens of the eastern woodrat (*Neotoma floridana*) in the woods near the mouth of the Osage River, in Osage and Calloway Counties. It was almost another month before they had pushed upstream far enough to reach the Kansas River, near which they saw Carolina parakeets and encountered two villages of Kansa natives.

They reached the present border of Nebraska on July 11, camping near the mouth of the Big Nemaha River on the Nebraska side and the Tarkio River on the Missouri side. By then they were traveling along the so-named bald-pated hills. These tall, loess-formed hills of western Iowa were covered at their lower levels by hardwood forests, but often were capped with native prairie. On July 12, a short distance upstream from the mouth of the Big Nemaha River, they observed some low "artificial" mounds representing the sites of old Native American burial grounds. On the morning of July 30 the group arrived at a high bluff on the Nebraska side that is now part of Fort Calhoun. There they camped for four days and held a council with the assembled chiefs of the Otoe-Missouria tribe. This council was the first held between the natives of the central Missouri Valley and the U.S. government, and the bluff was thus named Council Bluff. It later became the site of Camp Missouri, the first military post in Nebraska, subsequently renamed Fort Calhoun.

On August 13 the group passed Omaha Creek and camped at an old Omaha village that night. On August 16 they seined more than 1,000 fish of at least ten species at this "fishing camp," none of which Elliott Coues could identify with certainty on the basis of the names that the men used. Fish caught in the Nebraska-Iowa region and farther up the Missouri River did include some remarkably large catfish (see the Montana chapter in this book). They remained

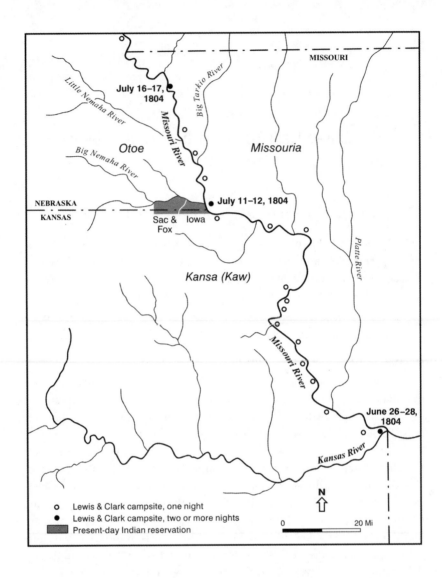

Map 1. Route of Lewis and Clark in Kansas and Missouri

OUTWARD ROUTE SCHEDULE: June 29 to September 7, 1804

RETURN SCHEDULE: August 29 to September 15, 1806

RIVER DISTANCE: Mouth of Kansas River to northernmost Nebraska–South Dakota boundary, estimated by Lewis and Clark as 691 river miles. Because of recent channelization and other river changes, the current distance is now substantially less.

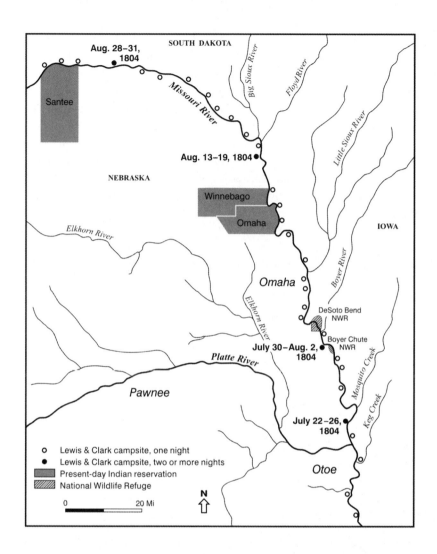

Map 2. Route of Lewis and Clark in Nebraska and Iowa

OUTWARD ROUTE SCHEDULE: June 29 to September 7, 1804

RETURN SCHEDULE: August 29 to September 15, 1806

RIVER DISTANCE: Mouth of Kansas River to northernmost Nebraska–South Dakota boundary, estimated by Lewis and Clark as 691 river miles. Because of recent channelization and other river changes, the current distance is now substantially less.

in the Omaha vicinity until August 19, and then began north again. On August 20, 1804, Sergeant Floyd died of a probable burst appendix and was buried on a high bluff just south of present-day Sioux City, Iowa. The next day the group passed the mouth of the Big Sioux River, camping in what is now Dakota County, Nebraska, with the South Dakota boundary on the opposite shore. The following day (August 22) they passed Ionia Creek and camped in what is now Union County, South Dakota. By September 7 they had passed out of what is now the shoreline of Boyd County, Nebraska, and were then entirely within the present boundaries of South Dakota.

The return trip was relatively rapid, the party arriving in what is now northern Boyd County, Nebraska, on August 29, 1806. They passed the mouths of the Niobrara, James, and Vermillion Rivers on September 1, 2, and 3, respectively. On September 8 they passed Council Bluff, and the next day the mouth of the Platte River. They passed the mouth of the Big Nemaha River and entered present-day Kansas on September 11. On September 15 they passed the mouth of the Kansas River and reentered Missouri. They reached the confluence of the Missouri and Mississippi Rivers on September 23, 1806, and were finally home.

# Mammals

### Badger *Taxidea taxus*

Near present-day Omaha–Council Bluffs a badger was killed on July 20, 1804. Another was brought into Fort Mandan by one of the party on January 18, 1805. The species was called a "brarow" by the expedition members. The Oglala branch of the Lakotas regarded the badger as having great strength and tenacity, and its symbolic powers extended to the healing of sick children.

### Beaver *Castor canadensis*

Beavers were first encountered on the outward journey near present-day Leavenworth, Kansas. They were seen again near Council Bluffs, Iowa, and after that were regularly encountered, being trapped at nearly every stopping point. In Montana alone they were reported from at least 33 locations. In his summary of the natural history of the expedition, Raymond Burroughs calculated that at least 113 beaver were killed over the entire expedition period. Three decades after the Lewis and Clark expedition, Maximilian, Prince of Wied, reported that in a single year 25,000 beaver pelts were brought into Fort Union. Beavers were already becoming rare only a decade later, when John J. Audubon visited the same fort. At the time of the Lewis and Clark expedition, North American beavers were highly valuable as pelts and were classified as the same species as the Old World beaver, but in 1820 they were recognized as separate types. After great overharvesting and near disappearance, the North American beaver has now recovered its former range and may be more common than at any time in the past century.

### Bison *Bison bison* FIG. 1

Bison were not encountered by Lewis and Clark until they had nearly reached the mouth of the Kansas River. A large herd of about 500 animals was observed on September 9 above the mouth of the Niobrara River, but none was killed until August 23, when they had they had reached the vicinity of present-day Vermillion, South Dakota. Burroughs calculated that at least 227 bison were killed during the expedition. The last known wild bison, in what is now North Dakota, was killed in 1888, a year after the last one in Montana was killed and about three years after the last Nebraska survivors were eliminated from the North Platte Valley.

### Black Bear *Ursus americanus* FIG. 2

Although several black bears were seen in Missouri, none was reported again in journal records until the party arrived in what is now North Dakota, when

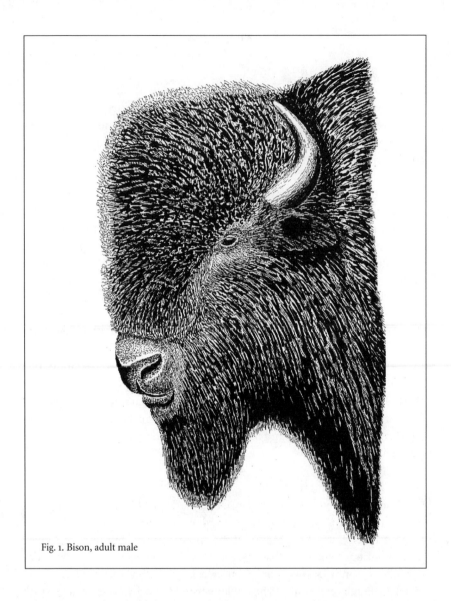

Fig. 1. Bison, adult male

a female and her cubs were seen near the mouth of the Little Missouri. In a letter to his mother, Captain Lewis mentioned seeing black bears in the Missouri Valley between Kansas and the mouth of the Big Sioux River. Farther west, no black bears were seen by Lewis and Clark between the mouth of the Little Missouri River and the Bitterroot Mountains of Montana, although grizzly bears were very common over this entire route. Burroughs calculated that at least 23

Fig. 2. Grizzly bear adult (top) and black bear adult (bottom)

black bears were killed during the expedition. Black bears are now completely gone from Kansas. They are also probably gone from the Missouri Valley of South Dakota (a 1968 Black Hills sighting is the most recent) and from North Dakota (there are some early-twentieth-century records of sightings in the Turtle Mountains). In 2000 a black bear wandered into northwestern Nebraska, perhaps from Wyoming, producing the first state record since 1907. Since then a few more bears have reported in western Nebraska.

### Eastern Fox Squirrel  *Sciurus niger*

Captain Clark reported that the fox squirrel was seen as far as about 20 miles upstream of the Niobrara River, in what is now extreme northern Nebraska (Boyd County) or adjacent southeastern South Dakota (Charles Mix County). However, fox squirrels were evidently seen to the north, at least to the vicinity of Fort Randall, South Dakota (noted on September 8, 1804).

### Elk  *Cervus elaphus*  FIG. 3

The first elk seen during the outward phase of the expedition was in the vicinity of Nishnabotna Creek, about 70 miles north of present-day St. Joseph, Missouri, along the present-day Kansas-Nebraska border. The first elk was killed when the party reached the vicinity of present-day Fort Calhoun, Nebraska. A second was shot at the mouth of the Little Sioux River, not much farther north, and a third near the mouth of the Niobrara River. From that point onward through the Dakotas and Montana, many more were killed. Burroughs calculated that at least 375 elk were killed during the expedition. On the return trip the last one was obtained near the mouth of the Kansas River. Eventually the elk was extirpated from Nebraska and both Dakotas. By 1877 it was gone from Nebraska, and from South Dakota by 1888. In North Dakota it survived into the 1890s. Captive herds now occur in all three states.

### Gray Squirrel  *Sciurus carolinensis*

Captain Clark reported that the gray squirrel was found as far north as the mouth of the Little Sioux River, in present-day Iowa (Harrison County) or adjacent Nebraska (Burt County).

### Pronghorn  *Antilocapra americana*  FIG. 4

Pronghorns were accurately described for the first time by Lewis and Clark, but they were not formally described and scientifically named until 1818. They were first observed on September 6, 1804, in the vicinity of the mouth of the Niobrara River. The first one was killed about a week later, in what is now southern South Dakota. Burroughs calculated that at least 62 pronghorns were killed during the expedition. By 1900 the pronghorn population in Nebraska had been reduced to about 100 animals, and by 1925 there were only about 225 in North Dakota. More recently it has recovered somewhat in Nebraska and also in the Dakotas.

### White-tailed Deer  *Odocoileus virginianus*

Deer of this common and widespread eastern species were seen from near the start of their expedition north and west to the Three Forks region of Montana.

Fig. 3. Elk, adult male

Burroughs calculated that at least 1,001 deer (including mule and black-tailed deer) were killed during the expedition. Deer were rather uniformly taken on the upstream phase from central Missouri to the Montana mountain ranges, and again on the return trip across the Great Plains. Usually the specific identity of the deer killed was not reported, but the expedition provided the first careful descriptions of both the mule deer of the Great Plains and the Pacific-slope

Fig. 4. Pronghorn, adult male

black-tailed deer (the two are now considered subspecies). The name "mule deer" was first coined by Captain Lewis.

## Birds

American Bittern  *Botaurus lentiginosus*
Captain Clark mentioned that the "Indian hen" was found as far upstream as the mouth of the Little Sioux River, in present-day northwestern Iowa or adja-

cent Nebraska. The vernacular name "Indian hen" was commonly used for this elusive species through the nineteenth century. Its population numbers have not changed significantly in the past four decades.

## American White Pelican  *Pelecanus erythrorhynchos*

On August 8, 1804, the expedition found a flock of several hundred white pelicans resting on a sandbar about two miles north of the mouth of Little Sioux River, in present-day Burt or Thurston County, Nebraska, and Monona County, Iowa. One of these birds was shot and measured by Captain Lewis, and its throat pouch was determined to hold five gallons of water. An estimate of 5,000 to 6,000 birds was made the same day by Private Whitehouse. Pelicans were also seen on the return trip, September 4 and 5, 1806, near the mouth of the Vermillion River, and within the river stretch from present-day Burt to Dixon Counties, Nebraska. A few were also shot on September 6 in what would become southern Burt County. A few white pelicans still use this dredged and highly channelized stretch of the Missouri River during migration to and from their North Dakota or Manitoba breeding grounds, but most migration now occurs in lakes and rivers farther west, where the waters may be clearer and less swift.

## (Black-bellied Plover  *Pluvialis squatarola*)

Myron Swenk speculated that some "plovers" seen by Captain Clark on August 15, 1804, in what is now Dakota County might have been migrating black-bellied plovers or perhaps American golden-plovers (*Pluvialis dominica*). Although both species migrate through Nebraska in autumn, the migration dates for the golden-plover are from early September to late November, and the black-bellied from August to early November. Thus, only the black-bellied would likely have been present in the state during mid-August. Other plover or sandpiper species are also possible candidates; Lewis and Clark apparently applied the term "plover" broadly to shorebirds, not necessarily to plovers specifically.

## Canada Goose  *Branta canadensis*

Large numbers of Canada geese were encountered between July 13, 1804, along the Richardson County shore, and September 6, 1804, along the present Nebraska–South Dakota boundary. Several of them were killed, including some well-grown goslings. Canada geese were later seen in at least 30 locations in Montana. On the return trip geese were also observed on September 4 and 5, 1806, between present-day Dixon and Burt Counties, Nebraska. Canada goose populations have increased significantly in North America during the last four decades, at least in part because the species is adjusting to the comforts of suburban living.

## Carolina Parakeet *Conuropsis carolinensis*

Captain Clark reported that this beautiful but now-extinct parakeet ("parotqueet") was seen all along the Missouri as far upstream as the Omaha ("Mahar") village, in what is now central Nebraska. Clark had also noted them earlier, near the mouth of the Kansas River, on June 26, 1804. The species was evidently extirpated from Nebraska by 1875 and it was last seen in South Dakota in 1884. The last specimen recorded in Kansas was one shot in 1904. The last known individual of the species died in the Cincinnati Zoo in 1914, where the last surviving passenger pigeon also died that same year.

## Cliff Swallow *Hirundo pyrrhonota*

This species must have been very common on the river during the upstream trip through Nebraska and South Dakota. The birds were seen nesting on July 16, 1804, near Sonora ("Sun") Island in present-day Nemaha County, and nests on a limestone cliff near Blackbird Hill (now Thurston County) were also noted. They were also found nesting along the shoreline of present-day Harrison County, Iowa, on August 5, 1804. Again, on August 22, a large number of nests were seen on a cliff along the shoreline of present-day Dixon County, Nebraska. The species now nests mostly on bridges, especially those made of concrete, which mimic cliff faces closely.

## Great Blue Heron *Ardea herodias*

Large numbers of these birds were seen on August 11, 1804, when the party camped on a sandbar above Blackbird Hill in present-day Thurston County, Nebraska. On August 30, 1804, in what is now western Cedar County, Nebraska, one tried to land on the mast of their keelboat and was captured. It was subsequently given to the local tribe of Yankton Sioux. Great blue heron populations have increased significantly in North America during the last four decades, perhaps in part because of improved protection of breeding colonies.

## Great Egret *Ardea alba*

A specimen of this egret was shot on August 2, 1804, at the site of present-day Fort Calhoun, Washington County. Great egrets have not historically nested along this stretch of the Missouri, but individual birds now often appear in late summer, after the breeding season. Like great blue herons, great egret populations have increased significantly in North America during the last four decades.

## Greater Prairie-chicken  *Tympanuchus cupido pinnatus*

Captain Clark referred to this species as "the Prairie fowl common to the Illinois" and said that its range extended as far north as the mouth of the James River, above which the sharp-tailed species occurred. The farthest point north at which Captain Clark saw the birds thus may have been in present-day Cedar County, Nebraska, or across the river on the South Dakota side near present-day Yankton. This interior race of the greater prairie-chicken is closely related to the now-extinct Atlantic coast race of prairie-chicken, which was called the heath hen (*T. c. cupido*). The interior race *pinnatus* thrived during the late 1800s as the fertile lands of the tallgrass prairies were initially opened to small-grain agriculture, but the population collapsed only a few decades later as natural breeding habitats became increasingly rare. The interior race has long been extirpated from the immediate Missouri Valley of Nebraska, but it does still occur as close as Johnson and Pawnee Counties near the Kansas-Nebraska border. It also still survives locally in the Missouri Valley of southern South Dakota, though it once ranged across essentially all of both Dakotas and even barely into eastern Montana.

## Interior Least Tern  *Sterna antillarum athalassos*  FIG. 5

A specimen of the least tern was shot in what is now Washington County, Nebraska, on August 5, 1804. Lewis carefully described it, and he should have been given full credit for discovering the species, but it was not formally described until 1843, from a specimen obtained in the West Indies. As with the piping plover, the middle Missouri River has long been a major nesting region for this subspecies, which is now nationally endangered. Like the piping plover, the least tern evolved in an environment adapted to falling water levels during late spring, rather than today's generally increasing water levels of the middle and lower Missouri River in the spring, when water is released from upstream dams to facilitate summer barge traffic.

## (Northern Harrier  *Circus cyaneus*)

This hawk was not identified as such by Lewis, but he referred to seeing (while on the Oregon coast) the "hen-hawk," a species of hawk with a "long tail and blue wings," calling it the same kind as that found farther east. The male northern harrier has bluish wings and a distinctly long tail, and has been tentatively identified as the species in question, rather than the much rarer peregrine falcon (*Falco peregrinus*). Since the harrier was not more specifically described as occurring in the Great Plains, it is not included as a positive occurrence.

Fig. 5. Least tern, adult and chick

## Piping Plover  *Charadrius melodus*  FIG. 6

Small plovers, described by Captain Clark as the "small species of Kildee," were observed to occupy river habitats as far upstream as the mouth of the Little Sioux River, present-day Burt County, Nebraska, or Harrison County, Iowa. It seems most likely that these birds were piping plovers, for which the middle Missouri River has long been a major breeding ground. However, the species was first officially described in 1824 on the Atlantic coast. The Great Plains population of piping plover is now nationally threatened.

## Red-tailed Hawk  *Buteo jamaicensis*

As with the northern harrier, this hawk was not identified as such by the expedition, but Captain Clark noted hawks along the shoreline of present-day Thurston and Burt Counties, which Swenk thought might have been this species. Since the red-tailed hawk is by far the most common breeding hawk of the central Missouri Valley, and is a permanent resident all the way north to North Dakota, it was almost certainly seen during the expedition's Great Plains phase. Red-tailed hawk populations have increased significantly in North America during the last four decades, the birds having benefited from improved federal protection and having learned to exploit foraging opportunities along superhighways.

## Red-winged Blackbird  (*Agelaius phoeniceus*)

Captain Clark observed large numbers of a "black bird" near Spirit Mound in Clay County, South Dakota (opposite Dixon County, Nebraska), on August 25,

Fig. 6. Piping plover, adult

1804. Swenk tentatively identified this species as the lark bunting (*Calamospiza melanocorys*). However, by August the lark bunting's breeding season is over, and males would be molting out of their nearly all-black breeding plumage and into a brown plumage. Other more common and permanently black-plumaged birds in that region are better possibilities, including various blackbirds and grackles. Gary Moulton has suggested that Clark observed the red-winged blackbird, which seems a much more likely choice, as by late August these abundant birds would be forming migratory flocks. One of the most numerous of North American songbirds, this species may number in excess of 100 million birds. However, although it probably increased greatly during the first half of the twentieth century, its overall population has been declining significantly over the past four decades as breeding habitats have been increasingly converted to agriculture.

## Ruffed Grouse *Bonasa umbellus*

Expedition members killed "several grous" during the time the group was camped just south of Council Bluffs in what is now Pottawattamie County, Iowa, on July 25, 1804. As Swenk concluded, these were almost certainly ruffed grouse rather than greater prairie-chickens or sharp-tailed grouse, given the wooded habitat along the river. Early records suggest that ruffed grouse once occurred along Nebraska's Missouri floodplain as far north as Omaha. They were extirpated from Nebraska and western Iowa by 1900.

(Whimbrel *Numenius phaeopus*
or Eskimo curlew *Numenius borealis*)

A shorebird called the "Jack Curloo" ("Jack" traditionally meaning small) was mentioned in a general way as having been seen by expedition members. It might be the whimbrel, a small curlew that was earlier known as the Hudsonian curlew. The even smaller Eskimo curlew also once migrated through the Great Plains in large numbers during spring, but it is now apparently extinct. Whimbrels still migrate in small numbers through the Great Plains but were unlikely to have been present during the expedition's passage up the Missouri River during the late summer of 1804, as their fall migration occurs mainly along the Atlantic coast. Whimbrels might also have been seen in eastern Montana the following spring, but they are now extremely rare in that state.

## Whip-poor-will *Caprimulgus vociferus*

Captain Clark heard whip-poor-wills calling on September 6, 1806, in the vicinity of present-day Blair, Nebraska, and he had also heard them earlier during the trip upstream through Missouri and Kansas. September is remarkably late for whip-poor-wills to call, as this species has usually finished vocalizing by early August. It has apparently moved gradually northward during the past two centuries and now breeds as far north as southern South Dakota. However, rangewide whip-poor-will populations have declined significantly across North America during the last four decades, as have populations of the ecologically similar common nighthawk (*Chordeiles minor*).

## Wild Turkey *Meleagris gallopavo*

Wild turkeys were killed and eaten by the expedition in Kansas and Nebraska. They were seen in large numbers on July 1, 1804, near present-day Leavenworth, Kansas, and one was killed on July 25, 1804, near present-day Council Bluffs. Another was killed the next day at the same camp, and others were taken on July 30 in what is now Washington County. Others were killed on August 5, 1804, on the Iowa side (now Harrison County) and one on August 9 on the Nebraska side (now Burt or Douglas County). Another was killed September 4 (now Knox County, Nebraska), and turkeys were seen above the mouth of the Niobrara River along the present Nebraska–South Dakota border (Boyd or Charles Mix County, respectively) on September 5. Others were killed in the same general boundary area on September 5 and 8. On the expedition's return trip through Nebraska wild turkeys were seen along the shorelines in present-day Nemaha and Richardson County. Although extirpated from the Missouri Valley of Nebraska and Kansas by shortly after the turn of the twentieth century, reintroduction efforts in both states have been successful. Wild turkey populations have increased significantly in North America during the last four decades, largely through releases and wildlife management practices.

## Wood Duck  *Aix sponsa*

The "summer duck" was quite familiar to Captain Lewis, who referred to it by that name on July 29, 1805, remarking that he had seen it as far west as the vicinity of Three Forks, Montana. However, unidentified ducks were also seen in some numbers during the river ascent through Nebraska, from as early as August 15, 1804 (present-day Dakota County), to September 5, 1804 (present-day Thurston or Burt County). As Swenk concluded, these most probably were wood ducks, which would have been common along the wooded Missouri River shorelines in late summer. Wood ducks were also reportedly seen in the vicinity of Great Falls, Montana, on June 19 and 23, 1805. Wood duck populations have increased significantly in North America during the last four decades, and their breeding range has expanded both to the west and north, partly as a result of the widespread erection of nesting boxes.

## Reptiles

## Bullsnake  *Pituophis catenifer*

One of these nonvenomous snakes was killed on the Iowa side of the Missouri River near Soldier Creek (now Harrison County, Iowa) on August 5, 1804, when it was seen near a colony of bank swallows (*Riparia riparia*). One was also killed in what is now Bon Homme County, South Dakota, on September 5, 1804.

## Plants

## Buffaloberry  *Shepherdia argentea*  FIG. 7

A widespread perennial shrub whose edible fruits were cooked or eaten raw by Native Americans. The fruits were used in feasts celebrating a girl's arrival at puberty, and the plant's English vernacular name relates to the fact that the berries were once used to flavor bison meat. Collected September 4, 1804, probably in present-day Niobrara County, Nebraska. A newly discovered species.

## Bur (Mossy-cup) Oak  *Quercus macrocarpa*

The most arid-adapted and fire-tolerant of the oaks on the northern plains. It produces fairly large acorns, a valuable food for many wildlife species as well as humans, who often boiled the acorns to rid them of bitter tannic acid. The abundant tannin in oak bark, acorns, and galls was almost certainly used by

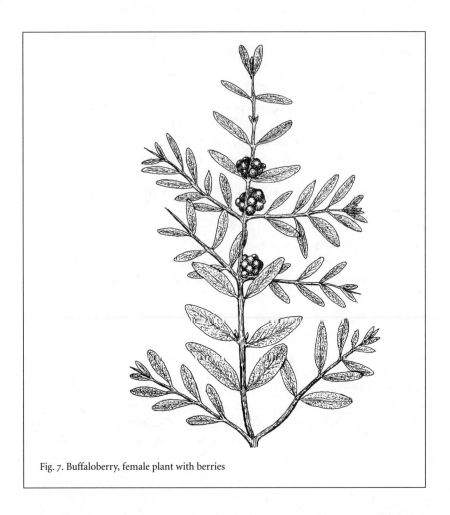

Fig. 7. Buffaloberry, female plant with berries

Native Americans for tanning leather. Collected September 5, 1804, probably in present-day Knox County, Nebraska.

## Curly-top Gumweed (Broad-leaved Gum Plant)
*Grindelia squarrosa*

A widespread, weedy and aromatic perennial. Its gummy secretions were used by Native Americans as a medicine for bronchitis, colic, and asthma, and its boiled leaves used as a poultice. Pawnees used a decoction from the flowering tops to treat saddle sores on horses. The flower extract is sometimes still used as an herbal medicine for treating whooping cough and asthma. Collected August 17, 1804, in present-day Dakota County, Nebraska.

## Horsetail (Scouring Rush) *Equisetum arvense*

This widespread herbaceous perennial is part of a genus of primitive plants having about eight species on the northern Great Plains. All have silica granules in their stems, making them effective for abrasive scouring. The Omaha–Ponca tribe thus used horsetails for smoothing bow wood. Collected August 10, 1804, in present-day Burt County, Nebraska.

## Meadow (Canada) Anemone *Anemone canadensis*

A widespread perennial forb that produces a glycoside (ranunculin) and saponins, which have reputed medicinal properties when applied externally. Its use was generally limited to medicine men, and its root was regarded as strong medicine by the Omaha-Poncas and many other northern tribes. Pregnant Blackfoot women drank a tea from the boiled plant to speed delivery. Collected August 17, 1804, in present-day Dakota County, Nebraska.

## Pasture Sagewort *Artemisia frigida* FIG. 8

A widespread perennial aromatic herb, used to bandage wounds, as toilet paper, for menstrual pads ("woman sage"), and to eliminate or at least cover the smell of dried meat. Collected September 2, 1804, probably in present-day Bon Homme County, South Dakota; also collected October 3, 1804, in present-day Porter or Sully County, South Dakota.

## Purple Prairie-clover *Petalostemon (Dalea) purpurea*

A widespread perennial forb. Native Americans steeped the bruised leaves and applied them to wounds, as Lewis noted on his original collection label. The roots were also chewed, and the stems were used for making brooms. Collected September 2, presumably in 1804, and probably in present-day Bon Homme County, South Dakota.

## Raccoon Grape (Simple-leaved Ampelopsis) *Ampelopsis cordata*

Like other grapes, the tiny fruits of this species are edible. Collected September 8, 1806, in present-day Washington County, Nebraska, and also September 14, 1806, in present-day Leavenworth County, Kansas.

## Rigid Goldenrod (Hard-leaved Goldenrod) *Solidago rigida*

The seeds of this widespread perennial forb species are often eaten by grouse and songbirds, and its flower heads are consumed by deer. Native American uses are not reported for this or other plains goldenrods. Collected September 12, 1806, in present-day Doniphan or Atchison County, Kansas, or Buchanan County, Missouri.

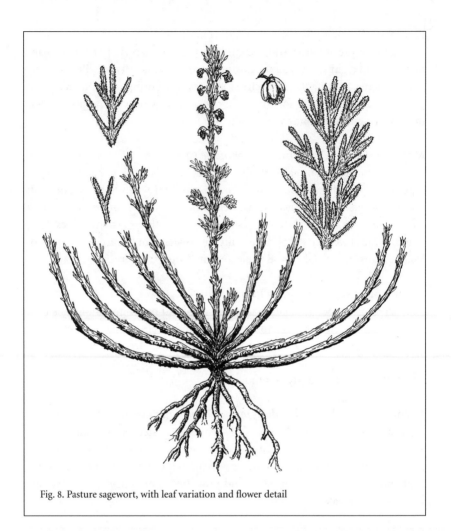

Fig. 8. Pasture sagewort, with leaf variation and flower detail

## Rocky Mountain Beeplant  *Cleome serrulata*

A widespread, weedy annual, with an odor that is very attractive to bees. Native Americans ate the leaves and tender stems, and boiled the stems to make syrup that could be dried and later eaten or used as a black pigment. The Lakotas and Assiniboine also made a "medicine" for attracting bison prior to hunting them, by pounding roots of beeplant and leadplant, and rubbing the resulting materials on their clothing. The abundant if small seeds were also ground into flour. Collected August 25, 1804, in present-day Cedar or Dixon County, Nebraska, or Clay County, South Dakota.

Wild Four-o'clock  *Mirabilis nyctaginea*

This is a widespread perennial forb whose vernacular name refers to the fact that it opens late in the afternoon, blooms all night, and wilts by the following morning. Its generic name means marvelous or strange, and its root was used by Native Americans for many medicinal purposes. The Lakotas boiled the root to treat fever, and it was also used as an apparently effective vermifuge. Among the Pawnees the dried root was ground up and used as a remedy for sore mouth in babies, and a root decoction was also used after childbirth to reduce swelling. The seeds and roots of at least some *Mirabilis* species contain the alkaloid trigonelline. Collected September 1, 1804, probably in present-day Bon Homme County, South Dakota; also collected October 3, 1804, in present-day Porter or Sully County, South Dakota.

Wild Rice  *Zizania palustris*

Wild rice has long been an important source of grain for Native Americans. It occurs from the Sandhills wetlands of central Nebraska north sporadically to North Dakota. Collected September 8, 1804, in present-day Boyd County, Nebraska, or (less probably) in Charles Mix or Gregory County, South Dakota. A newly discovered species.

Wild Rose  *Rosa arkansana*

A widespread native perennial shrub. The young shoots were used by Native Americans as a potherb, the petals were eaten raw, candied, or dried for use as perfume. The bark was smoked as a component of tobacco substitutes, and the leaves were used for tea or as decoctions to treat eye inflammations. The fruits ("hips") of roses are rich in vitamins A and C, as well as tannin, flavonol glycosides, and carotene. Collected September 5, 1804, in present-day Knox County, Nebraska, or in Charles Mix County, South Dakota. Also collected October 18, 1804, probably in present-day Sioux County, North Dakota.

# 3

# South Dakota and North Dakota

## Summary of Route and Major Biological Discoveries

Although the extreme southeastern boundary of South Dakota was reached on August 21, 1804, the first actual South Dakota campsite was made on August 23, when the group camped near the present site of Vermillion, South Dakota. On that same day they killed their first bison, near the present site of Ionia, Dixon County. On the 24th they passed a "bluff of blue clay," the so-called Burning Bluffs. The surface of this rocky outcrop was unaccountably warm to the touch, as if it had been burning from within, a phenomenon now believed to have been caused by chemical oxidation. By August 28 the group had reached the present site of Yankton, South Dakota, where they remained until August 31, holding a council with the local Yankton Sioux natives. On September 7 they observed a treeless dome on the south side of the river that they named "The Cupola" (now known as Old Baldy). At the base of this conical dome they discovered a colony of black-tailed prairie dogs, a species then new to science. After the entire group spent most of a day fetching and pouring about five barrels of water down one hole, the resident rodent was finally evicted and caught. Several others were shot and their skins preserved. Some prairie dogs were also eaten during the expedition and were considered fine table fare. Two other members of the prairie-dog community that directly depend on prairie dogs for their own survival, the burrowing owl (*Athene cunicularia*) and the black-footed ferret (*Mustela nigripes*), were not encountered. The ferret was not discovered and described scientifically for another half-century, but by 1900 it had already been virtually eliminated from North Dakota as well as from most of the Great Plains. It was one of the first Great Plains endemic species to be listed under the Endangered Species Act. The Great Plains race of the burrowing owl was discovered on the plains of western Nebraska in 1820. The rapidly declining burrowing owl may also soon be a candidate for similar nationally threatened or endangered listing.

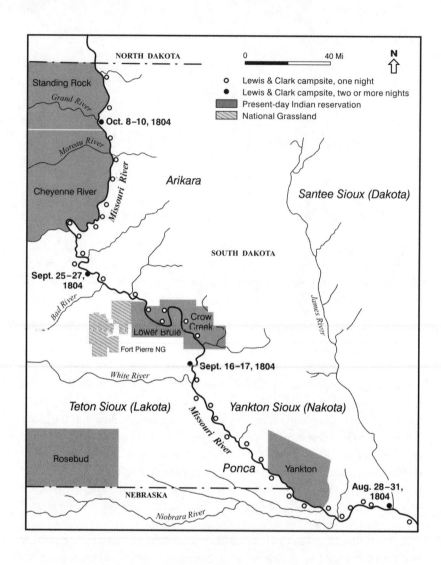

Map 3. Route of Lewis and Clark in South Dakota

OUTWARD ROUTE SCHEDULE: August 21, 1804, to April 27, 1805

RETURN SCHEDULE: August 3–5 to September 3, 1806

RIVER DISTANCE: Northernmost Nebraska–South Dakota boundary to present North Dakota–Montana boundary, estimated by Lewis and Clark as 830 miles. Because of recent impoundments and other river alterations, current river distances are substantially less than those encountered by Lewis and Clark.

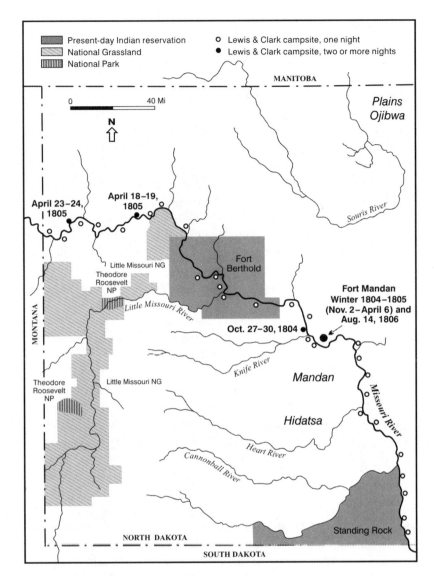

Map 4. Route of Lewis and Clark in North Dakota

OUTWARD ROUTE SCHEDULE: August 21, 1804, to April 27, 1805

RETURN SCHEDULE: August 3–5 to September 3, 1806

RIVER DISTANCE: Northernmost Nebraska–South Dakota boundary to present North Dakota–Montana boundary, estimated by Lewis and Clark as 830 miles. Because of recent impoundments and other river alterations, current river distances are substantially less than those encountered by Lewis and Clark. Clark estimated the total river distance from their starting point at Camp Wood to the Mandan villages as 1,500 miles, but it actually was closer to 1,600 miles.

The expedition left the common boundary of Nebraska and South Dakota on September 8, 1804. Moving north in South Dakota, large herds of bison were seen, as well as elk and deer. They passed the mouth of the White River on September 15, soon encountering "multitudes" of prairie dogs and vast herds of bison and antelope. By September 20 they had reached the Big Bend of the Missouri River, sending two men by horseback across the narrow peninsula to hunt and await their arrival around the enormous bend. Here the first female pronghorn was killed, as well as several mule deer. A coyote was also killed, and was identified as a small species of prairie wolf. On September 24 they reached what they called the "Teton" River (now known as the Bad River, its original English name), so named by the group because of the Teton (Brule) Lakotas who lived along it. Several days were spent interacting with this tribe, including some distinctly unfriendly encounters, and it was not until September 28 that they again departed upstream. They soon passed several abandoned villages of the Arikaras ("Rickaras"), and by October 8 met the first band of that group near the mouth of the Grand River. By the 13th they were on their way again, passing the mouth of Spring Creek (now Campbell County), a short distance below the present North Dakota boundary. That night was their last South Dakota campground, and on October 14 they camped near Blackfoot Creek, virtually on the present North Dakota–South Dakota boundary.

They passed the mouth of North Dakota's Cannonball River on October 18, in what is the present-day Standing Rock Reservation, and on the 19th counted 53 herds of bison and 3 elk herds, all in view at a single time. They soon began to encounter abandoned Mandan villages as well as old Arikara villages. There were also active Awatixa Hidatsa ("Minnetaree") villages in the area, along the Knife River. It was at one of these Hidatsa villages that the teenaged Shoshone woman Sacagawea was living with a French fur trader, Touissant Charbonneau. She had been captured and abducted near Three Forks about five years earlier by the Hidatsas, and had been won by Charbonneau on a wager. On October 26 Lewis and Clark arrived at an active Mandan village site, a location they selected for their winter quarters and named Fort Mandan. Later known as Fort Clark, it was located in what is now the southeastern corner of Mercer County. They were approximately 1,600 river miles up the Missouri from their starting point and roughly halfway across their transcontinental route.

The expedition spent the winter of 1804–5 at Fort Mandan, not departing again until April 7, 1805. At that point the Corps of Discovery consisted of 32 persons. Besides their basic exploratory party of 28 men, they had added 2 interpreters, including Touissant Charbonneau as well as Sacagawea and her infant son, Baptiste, born only about two months previously. The keelboat and its crew of eleven men were sent back to St. Louis, along with many specimens and artifacts that were destined for Washington DC. Among them were live prairie dogs and magpies, 60 preserved plant specimens, a variety of Native American materials, and various skins and skeletons.

The Corps then headed upstream, passing the mouth of the Little Missouri River on April 12 and reaching the mouth of the Yellowstone River on April 26, where they were only a few miles from the present-day boundary of Montana. Between this point and the present boundary, Fort Union was built in 1830 and operated as a frontier trading post for some time before being abandoned. They entered what is now eastern Montana on April 27, 1805, camping just a few miles upstream.

The return trip was much more rapid and far less rewarding in terms of biological discovery. Little time was wasted during this phase, especially after Captain Lewis's narrow escape from eight Blackfoot men during his independent exploration of the upper Marias River of western Montana, together with three of his men. After that hazardous encounter the four men quickly returned to the Missouri River. There they rejoined the rest of their party and continued downstream, reaching the mouth of the Yellowstone River and the approximate boundary of present-day North Dakota on August 7.

This confluence of the Yellowstone and Missouri Rivers (approximately at the current Montana–North Dakota border) was the agreed-upon rendezvous point for rejoining Captain Clark and his men after their separate route down the Yellowstone River. However, by the time Lewis and his party finally arrived at the planned meeting point, Clark's group had already departed downstream and had left an explanatory note. Lewis and his men thus moved quickly downstream to catch up. Lewis's party finally caught up with that of Captain Clark about 150 miles below the mouth of the Yellowstone River on August 12, 1806, at a location now flooded by Lake Sakakawea but that was probably near Crow Flies High Butte.

The combined Corps then descended the Missouri River in what is now North Dakota. They passed the mouth of the Little Missouri River on August 13, and reached Fort Mandan by the 17th. On August 22 they passed the mouth of the Grand River, and thus were about 25 miles into present-day South Dakota, and on August 25th they passed the mouth of the Cheyenne River. By September 1 they had passed the mouth of the Niobrara River, and had the present-day Nebraska shoreline on their south side. On September 4th they passed the mouth of the Big Sioux River, and were then entirely out of South Dakota and had entered what would eventually become Iowa and Nebraska.

## Mammals

### Bighorn Sheep  *Ovis canadensis auduboni*  FIG. 9

This species was not encountered until April 26, 1805, at the mouth of the Yellowstone River, where several were seen during a hike a few miles up the Yellowstone. Earlier in Fort Mandan the horns from two animals were obtained, and Captain Clark noted that they were called "rock mountain sheep" by the French. The Great Plains population was later (1901) described as representing a distinct race, and was named by C. Hart Merriam after J. J. Audubon, based on a specimen from the Missouri Valley of South Dakota. It became extinct only a decade or two after it was initially named.

### Bison  *Bison bison*

As noted earlier, the first large herd of bison was noted on September 9, 1804, near the mouth of the Niobrara River along the Nebraska–South Dakota boundary. Thereafter, bison were present in uncountable numbers on the Dakota plains. On September 17, 1804, near the mouth of the White River, a group of about 3,000 were in view at a single time. Between the vicinity of Bon Homme Island, South Dakota, and the expedition's arrival at Fort Mandan, 35 bison were killed. One more was killed at Fort Mandan in November, and at least 42 more by the middle of December. Only three were killed during the rest of winter at Fort Mandan, and the animals were not mentioned again until the group began their spring ascent up the Missouri. Then, from about 50 miles north of the Little Missouri River, increasing numbers of bison were seen, including "immence herds" of bison, deer, and pronghorns in the vicinity of White Earth River on April 22, 1805.

### Black-tailed Prairie Dog  *Cynomys ludovicianus*  FIG. 10

The black-tailed prairie dog was first described by Lewis and Clark but not formally named as a new species until 1815. As noted earlier, it was discovered somewhat upstream of the mouth of the Niobrara River on September 7, 1804, at a clay promontory the explorers described as "The Tower," located in what is now northern Boyd County. The animals were called "barking squirrels" by Captain Lewis, and prairie dogs (a rough translation of the French *petite chien*) by Captain Clark. The description by Captain Lewis is highly detailed and accurate; that of Captain Clark is shorter but very interesting. The explorers also saw prairie-dog towns in South Dakota near the White River. These rodents were not specifically mentioned while the expedition was in North Dakota, although the animals are known from later records to have been abundant along the Missouri River, and the four prairie dogs sent back to Washington DC in the

Fig. 9. Bighorn, adult male

spring of 1805 from Fort Mandan probably had been captured locally. One of them survived the 4,000-mile journey and was exhibited for a time at Charles W. Peale's Philadelphia Museum, then located in Independence Hall. Prairie dogs were again observed in Montana, including a colony about seven miles in length that was seen in the vicinity of the mouth of the Marias River. At that location a few were killed and eaten, and were found to be "well flavoured and tender." They were also seen near the mouth of the Musselshell River. On the return trip prairie dogs were seen as far south as the vicinity of the Niobrara River, along the South Dakota–Nebraska border, and apparently close to where they had first been discovered.

### Coyote  *Canis latrans*  FIG. 11

Lewis and Clark deserve credit for discovering that this species is distinct from the larger gray wolf. Captain Clark first mentioned it on September 18, 1804, when a "prairie wolf" said to be the size of a gray fox was shot near the White River of South Dakota. Clark had earlier (August 12, 1804) observed a

Fig. 10. Black-tailed prairie dog, adult ("all-clear" or "jump-yip" call)

kind of smaller wolf that "barks like a large ferce dog." It wasn't until the expedition was on the Missouri River the next spring (May 5, 1805) that Clark found a den of young "wolves," and Captain Lewis referred to them as being a "small wolf or burrowing dog of the prairies." Lewis noted their doglike vocalizations, their relatively long and pointed ears, and their unusually long claws. Although

Fig. 11. Coyote, adult

the coyote was thus first well described by Lewis and Clark, it was not formally named as a distinct species until 1828.

### Eastern Cottontail  *Sylvilagus floridanus*

Unidentified rabbits were seen in present-day South Dakota between the Niobrara and White Rivers, near the mouth of the White River, and again in the Big Bend area. These sightings have logically been attributed to the eastern cottontail, although the present-day range of the desert cottontail (*S. audubonii*) also rather closely approaches the Missouri River in central South Dakota.

### Gray Wolf  *Canis lupus*  FIG. 12

The prairie race (*nubilis*) of the gray wolf was first described in detail by Lewis and Clark, but it was not formally named until 1823. The gray wolf was apparently first encountered on July 20, 1804, near the mouth of Weeping Water Creek in southeastern Nebraska, when a "large yellow wolf" was killed. On

Fig. 12. Gray wolf, adult

September 21, near the Big Bend of the Missouri in South Dakota, a "white" wolf was shot and skinned. Both wolves and coyotes were seen during the expedition between southeastern Nebraska and the Pacific Coast; both were called "wolves" and often were not distinguished. However, the larger form was sometimes called the "white wolf" and at other times the "large brown wolf." Near Wolf Point, Montana, on May 5, 1805, Captain Lewis described the wolf well, pointing out that it differed from the smaller coyote in not taking refuge in the ground or in a burrow. He also noted that the colors of true wolves varied from blackish brown or gray to creamy white. Wolves were eliminated from Nebraska by 1920, from North Dakota probably during the 1920s, and from South Dakota by 1934, when the last one was killed in the Black Hills. Vagrants have been reported at least three times in North Dakota since 1980.

## Grizzly Bear *Ursus arctos* FIG. 2

The grizzly bear was first mentioned by the expedition about 25 miles below the mouth of the Niobrara River, along the Nebraska–South Dakota boundary, where a "White Bear Clift" was named as the site where a grizzly bear had once been killed. Bear tracks were seen on October 7, 1804, on Fox Island, near the mouth of the Moreau River in South Dakota. However, the first actual encounter with a grizzly was on October 20, 1804, when one was wounded near the mouth of the Heart River, just south of present-day Bismarck, North Dakota. Bear tracks of great size were also encountered at the mouth of the Little Missouri River on April 13, 1805. Finally, a grizzly bear was killed by Captain Lewis on April 29 at the mouth of the Yellowstone River, near the Montana border. An even larger male was killed by Captain Clark on May 5; this preserved specimen was the basis for a later formal description and naming (*Ursus ferox*) of the species. When Prince Maximilian and Audubon visited the Fort Union area 30 and 39 years later, respectively, grizzly bears were still common there. However, grizzly bears were extirpated from South Dakota by about 1890 and from North Dakota by about the end of the nineteenth century. Two were killed near Oakdale, North Dakota, in the autumn of 1897, perhaps representing the last known from that state, or indeed from anywhere within the Great Plains east of Montana.

## Long-tailed Weasel *Mustela frenata*

Lewis and Clark did not mention seeing live weasels in the Great Plains, but Captain Lewis purchased a weasel skin at a Mandan village in November 1804. Although weasel skins, especially the white winter-pelage type (ermine), were much prized by Native Americans for their decorative value, they had no real market value for white trappers, and thus no numerical records of early weasel skin harvests are available.

## (Lynx *Felis lynx*
## or Bobcat *Felis rufus*)

Although bobcats are still common in western North Dakota, there is no record of live bobcats having been encountered by the expedition. Captain Clark mentioned having acquired gloves and a cap made of the skin of a "louservia." Such skins were obtained from the Mandans. Lynxes were also moderately regular in northeastern North Dakota during the early 1800s, but they were often confused with bobcats. Maximilian reported in 1833 that 1,000 to 2,000 lynx skins were brought into Fort Union annually, as well as a similar number of bobcat skins. Vagrant lynx still occasionally wander into northern North Dakota from Canada.

## (Meadow Vole *Microtis pennsylvanica*)

Rodents, possibly meadow voles, were mentioned by Captain Lewis as gathering seed hordes of "artichokes" (probably *Helianthus tuberosus*). However, Rueben Thwaites has suggested that these rodents might instead have been "gophers" (his usage presumably referring to ground squirrels rather than true gophers).

## Mule Deer  *Odocoileus hemionus*  FIG. 13

The mule deer was first recognized and accurately described by Lewis and Clark but not formally described until 1817. It was first mentioned on September 5, in the vicinity of the Niobrara River, when the descriptive term "black-tailed deer" was applied to several deer seen by one of the crew members. The first specimen of this species was shot near the mouth of the White River, South Dakota, on September 17, 1804. Captain Clark immediately recognized it to be different from the white-tailed deer, especially in its large and long ears, its more rounded and black-tipped tail, and in its distinctive bounding behavior when frightened. Four more were shot near the Big Bend of the Missouri on September 19, when the equally characteristic symmetrical forking pattern of the species' antlers was also noted by Captain Clark. A much more detailed anatomical description was provided by Captain Lewis on May 10, 1805, when he initially referred to it as a "mule deer," as distinct from the white-tailed or "common deer." Relatively few mule deer were mentioned during the North Dakota phase of the trip. During the return trip mule deer were last noted in the vicinity of the White River, South Dakota.

## Muskrat  *Fiber zibethicus*

Muskrats were mentioned only briefly in the expedition journals (e.g., August 7, 1805), but in contrast to beaver no special note was made of these familiar and relatively valueless animals, at least as to their pelt values.

## Northern River Otter  *Lontra canadensis*

River otters were first reported by the expedition in the vicinity of present-day Bismarck on October 22, 1804, when one was killed. It was next noted on

Fig. 13. Mule deer, adult male (in autumn)

April 14, 1805, when one was seen near the mouth of the Little Missouri River in northwestern North Dakota. In 1833 Maximilian reported that 200 to 300 otter skins were brought in annually to Fort Union, and the skins were often used by Native Americans as decorations. By the early 1900s otters had been eliminated from all Nebraska rivers and were very rare in South Dakota and North Dakota. Transplant and release efforts in Nebraska have helped restore that state's population, which is still very small. There have been recent records of otters in four South Dakota counties as well.

### Porcupine *Erethizon dorsatum*

A few mentions of the porcupine appear in the journals. Like the muskrat, it was evidently not considered to be of special economic or biological interest. One was killed near present-day Brule City, South Dakota, on September 13, 1804, and others were seen near present-day Poplar, Montana, on May 5, 1805, where a small river was named Porcupine River (now the Poplar River) because of the abundance of porcupines there.

### Pronghorn *Antilocapra americana*

The first pronghorn killed during the expedition was obtained near the mouth of the White River in South Dakota on September 14, 1804. This was a male, or "Buck Goat," in Captain Clark's words. He described it fairly well, concluding it to be "more like the Antilope or Gazella of Africa" than like any species of goat. The first female was killed six days later in the Big Bend region of South Dakota. Clark noted the female's smaller size and smaller horns, and that neither sex has a beard. He thought the animals to be "keenly made" and "butifull." Pronghorns were eventually almost extirpated from Nebraska by the early 1900s but have recently become locally reestablished as a result of release programs. They were also barely surviving in the Dakotas by the turn of the twentieth century but have recovered well in those two states.

### Richardson's Ground Squirrel *Spermophilus richardsonii* FIG. 14

There is no hard evidence that Lewis and Clark discovered this fairly common Great Plains species, but it is likely that the ground squirrel they observed near the vicinity of present-day Garrison Dam on April 9, 1805, was of this species. The species is still so common in North Dakota that that state has at times been called the "Flickertail State." However, no clear and convincing description of the animal was provided by either Lewis or Clark. The Richardson's ground squirrel was not formally described until 1811.

### Short-tailed Shrew *Blarina brevicauda*

Some specimens of "mice" that were shipped from Fort Mandan to President Jefferson were evidently shrews. These were later identified as probably being short-tailed shrews, but the specimens since have been lost.

### Striped Skunk *Mephitis mephitis*

The only mention of this species in the Great Plains was a comment made by Lewis as to seeing a "pole-cat" near the mouth of the White River in South Dakota. Another was seen near the mouth of the Musselshell River in Montana on May 25, 1805. The Lakotas honored the skunk for its refusal to retreat in the

Fig. 14. Richardson's ground squirrel, adult ("picket-pin" posture)

face of danger, and sometimes their chiefs tied the skins of skunks to their heels to symbolize the fact that they never ran from a battle. Like the badger, wolf, and fox, the skunk possessed special symbolic powers to the tribes of the high plains.

(Swift Fox  *Vulpes velox*)

The tiny swift fox was evidently not noticed by Lewis and Clark while they were in North Dakota, but only a few decades later Maximilian reported this species ("prairie foxes") to be common around Fort Clark, and kept one as a pet. Still later, Audubon also found them to be common at both Fort Clark and Fort Union. One that had been captured alive at Fort Clark was presented to Audubon, and he also kept it as a pet, eventually taking it back to his home in New York State. Swift fox skins were worn by men of the Kit Fox Society of the

Oglala Sioux, and their fur was additionally used to wrap war lances. Similarly, wolf skins were worn ceremonially by men of the Wolf Society and were also used as camouflage when stalking bison. The Kit Fox Society of the Oglalas was one of the "policing" societies largely concerned with camp life and hunting, whereas the Wolf Society was a war society. However, inherent courage was also a part of the Kit Fox Society, and according to Joseph Brown one of their songs was as follows: "I am a Fox. I am supposed to die. If there is anything difficult, if there is anything dangerous, that is mine to do."

### White-tailed Jackrabbit *Lepus townsendii* FIG. 15

The white-tailed jackrabbit was first described by Lewis and Clark but was not formally described and scientifically named until 1839. Lewis and Clark properly referred to jackrabbits as "hares" rather than rabbits. After collecting the first specimen near the mouth of the White River on September 14, 1804, Captain Clark provided measurements and commented on its white tail. His description thus clearly separates it from the black-tailed jackrabbit (*L. californicus*) of the same general region, although it now generally occurs farther south. Other sightings of jackrabbits in South Dakota occurred on September 17, 20, and 24, 1804. One was killed at Fort Mandan in January of 1805, and another was obtained in North Dakota the following spring, not far north of Fort Mandan. Jackrabbits were also seen at several Montana sites. One that was shot on May 26, 1805, weighed 8.5 pounds, which is fairly large even for a white-tailed jackrabbit, and is substantially larger than the black-tailed jackrabbit. White-tailed jackrabbits remained common in North Dakota well into the 1900s; during one organized hunt near the town of New England in December of 1924, 7,550 of the animals were killed. This writer remembers community hunts being organized in the Red River Valley of North Dakota into the mid-1930s, during the depression and drought years. White-tailed jackrabbits are now quite rare in the Dakotas and Nebraska.

### Birds

### American Crow *Corvus brachyrhynchos*

Although crows must have been seen frequently across the Great Plains, little note of them was made. In the expedition's Meteorological Register of April 9, 1805, it was noted that crows had returned to Fort Mandan. Crows were also noted in some Montana locations, such as near Great Falls (June 15, 1805) and along the upper Marias River (July 19, 1806). American crow populations have increased significantly in North America during the last four decades, as the birds have benefited from better protection and from adjustments to city life.

Fig. 15. White-tailed jackrabbit, adult in summer pelage

### American Kestrel  *Falco sparverius*

This common and widespread small falcon, traditionally called a "sparrow hawk," was observed in the vicinity of the Little Missouri River on April 13, 1805. It was probably too common and too familiar for Lewis and Clark to have made repeated mention.

### American Robin  *Turdus migratorius*

Few specific notes were made on this common species. In the expedition's Meteorological Register of April 22, 1805, it was noted that robins had returned to Fort Mandan. Robins were also seen near Great Falls, Montana (June 15, 1805), and on the upper Marias River (July 19, 1806). American robin populations have increased significantly in North America during the last four decades, probably at least in part through increased bird-feeding by humans.

### Bald Eagle  *Haliaeetus leucocephalus*

Eagles of unspecified species were noted as far downstream as the vicinity of the mouth of the Niobrara River on September 5, 1806. Bald eagles were first specifically mentioned on April 10, 1805, when they were observed nesting in tall cottonwood trees between Fort Mandan and the Little Missouri River. Other eagle nests were noted on April 25, April 27, and May 7, 1805, near the mouth of the Yellowstone River. On May 8 they were first observed to have young in the nests, and the birds were again seen on August 9 at the mouth of Prairie Creek, near Grayling, Montana. Long on the federally endangered list, the bald eagle has recovered significantly in the past few decades as a result of intensive management efforts, and now breeds in both the Missouri and Yellowstone Valleys of Montana.

### Bank Swallow  *Riparia riparia*

Captain Clark saw a "vast number" of "a small brown martin" catching insects above Spirit Mound, South Dakota, on August 25, 1804. These were most likely bank swallows but might have included rough-winged swallows (*Stelgidopteryx serripennis*), which also nest along the steep bluffs of the Missouri River. Both species would have been gathering for fall migration during late August. Bank swallows historically nested in vast numbers on the nearly vertical loess bluffs along the middle Missouri River, from the mouth of the Platte into South Dakota, according to James Ducey. Recent population trends of these species are not clear.

### Black-billed Magpie  *Pica pica*

Magpies were apparently first seen near the Big Bend of the Missouri and were later found to be winter residents of Fort Mandan. Four living specimens were sent from Fort Mandan to President Jefferson, who in turn passed at least one surviving individual on to Charles W. Peale for exhibit in the Philadelphia Museum. This specimen was later used by Alexander Wilson as the basis for an illustration in his *American Ornithology*. The species was already well known from Europe, but the American magpie represented a new subspecies. Magpies were also reported in eastern Montana near Fort Union (April 27, 1805) and near Fort Peck (August 3, 1806). Black-billed magpie populations have decreased significantly in North America during the last four decades.

### Blue Jay  *Cyanocitta cristata*

Although the blue jay is not mentioned in the journals, one of the expedition members informed Wilson (*American Ornithology*) that the generally ubiquitous blue jay was progressively replaced by the magpie to the north and west of the Big Bend of the Missouri River, where the magpie was first encountered (Reid and Gannon 1999). This same sort of ecological and geographic replacement of the blue jay by the magpie is evident today on the western high plains.

Like magpies, blue jay populations have declined significantly in North America during the last four decades, perhaps in part because of competition with the larger American crows.

### Cedar Waxwing *Bombycilla cedrorum*

A flock of "cherry or cedar-birds" was seen near Fort Mandan on April 6, 1805, and several were killed. This rather common songbird of the northern forests and riparian woodlands was not mentioned again.

### Common Poorwill *Phalaenoptilus nuttallii* FIG. 16

On October 16, 1804, in what is now southern North Dakota, Captain Lewis captured a small bird that he recognized as belonging to the "order of the [blank space; he probably intended "Caprimulgiformes"] or goat sucker." He noted that the bird appeared to be becoming dormant—a fact that was not fully established for this or any other North American bird species by ornithologists for another 145 years. Lewis also astutely observed that under the freezing conditions (30 degrees F) the bird could scarcely move, and that even after its heart and lungs were pierced with a knife it remained alive for nearly two hours! Like his later substantiated report of finding Canada geese nesting in trees (probably using old nests of osprey or eagle), this observation was probably not believed by scientists of the time.

### Common Raven *Corvus corax*

Ravens wintered in immense numbers in the vicinity of Fort Mandan. They were also seen at various times farther west in Montana, for example, near the present-day sites of Missoula (August 1, 1806) and Lincoln (August 6, 1806) and on the upper Marias River (July 19, 1806). Just as magpies tend to replace blue jays as one proceeds westward in the Great Plains, ravens also tend to replace crows in the same geographic manner. Common raven populations have increased significantly in North America during the last four decades.

### (Franklin's Gull *Larus pipixcan* and Forster's Tern *Sterna forsteri*)

No definite evidence of either of these species appears in the journals, although white gulls were mentioned at various times. On August 7, 1806, near the mouth of the Yellowstone River, Lewis reported flocks of "white gulls about the size of a pigeon, with the top of their heads black." This description might fit the Franklin's gull better than the Forster's tern, since the gull is more likely to migrate in large flocks, and in the summer plumage of the Franklin's gull the entire upper and rear parts of the head are black or dark gray.

Fig. 16. Common poorwill, adult

### Golden Eagle *Aquila chrysaetos* FIG. 17

This is the "grey eagle" of Lewis and Clark, who also at times called it the "beautiful eagle" or "calumet bird." A calumet is the long-stemmed ceremonial pipe used by Native Americans, and the bicolored tail feathers of golden eagles were often used to adorn such pipes. Golden eagles were one of the few birds wintering in the vicinity of Fort Mandan, according to Lewis's notes of April 8, 1805. Several "very large grey" eagles were again seen on July 11, 1805, near Great Falls, Montana. One was also seen at the mouth of the Musselshell River in Montana on August 3, 1806, during the return trip.

### Great Horned Owl *Bubo virginianus*

Captain Lewis reported that on April 14, 1805, the group shot a "large hooting owl." He believed it to be more "booted" (an ornithological term meaning that there are feathers on the lower leg or tarsus) and more generally feathered than the eastern form of this species. This is an interesting (albeit incorrect) ornithological point that testifies to Lewis's keen scientific interests.

### Hairy Woodpecker *Picoides villosus*
### or Downy Woodpecker *P. pubescens*

No specific mention was made of these fairly widespread species. In the expedition's Meteorological Register of February 8, 1805, it was noted that the "black-and-white speckled woodpecker" had returned to Fort Mandan. The

Fig. 17. Golden eagle, adult

larger hairy woodpecker is more likely to be found in North Dakota during February than is the downy, although the downy is perhaps generally somewhat more common than the hairy as a breeding species along the upper Missouri Valley. A hairy or downy woodpecker was also seen upstream from the mouth of the Musselshell River on May 18, 1805, in Montana.

### Horned Lark  *Eremophila alpestris*

This species, which Captain Clark called the "ren or Prairie burd," was seen in "great numbers" near Spirit Mound in what is now Clay County, South Dakota, on August 25, 1804. This species was also noted to have returned seasonally to western North Dakota by April 10, 1805. Horned larks were again seen near Great Falls, Montana (June 19–25, 1805). They are still among the most common breeding birds of the shortgrass plains and are one of the few likely to overwinter as far north as North Dakota and Montana. Although called a "ren," the bird's seasonal timing and habitats as described by Lewis and Clark do not fit the house wren (*Troglodytes aedon*). Horned lark populations have decreased significantly in North America during the last four decades as grassland habitats have declined.

### Killdeer  *Charadrius vociferus*

The "Kildee" was apparently well known to Lewis and Clark but was specifically mentioned only once in the Great Plains region. Lewis noted it on April 8, 1805, in the vicinity of the Knife River in North Dakota.

### Long-billed Curlew  *Numenius americanus*

On April 17, 1805, in northwestern North Dakota, the group saw a "curlue." A "brown curlue" was also noted on April 22, 1805, near the present Montana border. These most probably were long-billed curlews, as the smaller and arctic-nesting whimbrel (*Numenius phaeopus*) is very rare in Montana. Birds described as curlews were also later seen in Montana during the nesting season, near Great Falls (July 11–13, 1805) and near the present locations of Townsend (July 24, 1805) and Whitehall (August 3, 1805), all within the historic breeding range of long-billed curlews. Long-billed curlew populations have declined significantly in North America during the last four decades; these birds need large areas of native grasslands for breeding.

### Northern Flicker  *Colaptes auratus*

In Lewis's Meteorological Notes of April 11, 1805, he reported the spring arrival of the well-known "lark-woodpecker." His description perfectly fits the yellow-shafted form of the northern flicker. About four decades later, Audubon encountered flickers that were intermediate in plumage between the eastern yellow-shafted and western red-shafted types, along this same part of the upper Missouri Valley. At the time, the red-shafted was considered a separate species from the yellow-shafted, but they are now regarded as only racially distinct, as a broad zone of intermingled genetic types occurs in this general plains region. Northern flicker populations have declined significantly in North America during the last four decades, as have at least two other woodpecker species.

### Passenger Pigeon  *Ectopistes migratorius*

This now-extinct but once extremely common pigeon was first mentioned on February 12, 1804, near the mouth of the Missouri River at the start of their trip. Captain Lewis mentioned the birds again near the White River in southern South Dakota on September 16, 1804. They were also seen in west-central

Montana on July 12 and 13, 1805, near the mouth of the Sun River, and one was shot by Captain Lewis on the 13th. On the return trip Lewis noted them near Missoula on July 5, 1806, and also along Cut Bank River in northwestern Montana on July 25, 1806. Captain Clark likewise mentioned seeing pigeons along the Yellowstone River on July 25, 1806. These latter sightings may well have involved the band-tailed pigeon (*Columba fasciata*), as the passenger pigeon is only known with certainty to have occurred in northern Montana. The passenger pigeon was last reported from the Montana region in 1875, from what is now South Dakota in 1884, and from North Dakota in 1892. The last wild birds observed anywhere were seen about 1900, and the last-known individual died in captivity in 1914.

### Plains Sharp-tailed Grouse *Tympanuchus phasianellus jamesi* FIG. 18

Sharp-tailed "grows," also called "pointed tail Prairie fowl" by Captain Clark, were observed to "commence" at the mouth of the James River, and they were seen from "the Big bend upwards." They were observed later at Fort Mandan, North Dakota (February 13, 1805), and again near the mouth of the Little Missouri River in extreme western North Dakota (April 12, 1805). On April 15, 1805, about 50 miles above the mouth of the Little Missouri River and close to the present day Montana border, a group of displaying males was seen by Captain Lewis. Farther west in Montana sharp-tailed grouse were also seen near the mouth of the Musselshell River (May 21–22, 1805) and near present-day Missoula (July 2, 1806). Lewis and Clark were the first biologists to encounter and mention what are now recognized as the plains (*jamesi*) and Columbian (*columbianus*) races of the sharp-tailed grouse. Sharp-tailed grouse of the plains race *jamesi* still occur over much of the high plains region, although the more western race *columbianus* is declining as a serious rate and is locally endangered or extirpated in many areas.

### Snow Goose *Chen caerulescens*

Captain Lewis reported "great numbers" and "large flocks" of "white brant" on April 9 and 13, 1805, between Fort Mandan and the Little Missouri River, and again on May 5, near Prairie Elk Creek. The ones he described were of the usual white-plumaged morph type; the "gray brant" he described as also present in the flocks might have been young of the previous year or perhaps adults or young of the so-called "blue goose" genetic variant, which are mostly dark grayish brown. He also described a "common brown brant" two-thirds the size of the "common goose" (Canada goose), which might have been one of the smaller races of the Canada goose. The "pided" (pied) brant seen and carefully described later in Oregon was the greater white-fronted goose (*Anser*

Fig. 18. Sharp-tailed grouse, adult male

*albifrons*), which also migrates through the Great Plains in large numbers. In Montana snow geese were reportedly seen as far west as the vicinity of Wolf Point (May 5, 1805). Snow goose populations have increased very significantly in North America during the last four decades, largely because they have adjusted their migrations to exploit the protection afforded by wildlife refuges, and are now perhaps more abundant than at any time in American history.

Trumpeter Swan  *Cygnus buccinator*  FIG. 19

Captain Lewis observed wild swans between Ford Mandan and the Yellowstone River in the spring (April) of 1805. These might have been migrating tundra (previously whistling) swans, but perhaps more likely were trumpeter swans, quasi-permanent residents of the northern plains. Later, Captain Lewis described the whistling swan in some detail, based on his observations in Oregon, and was the first person to call it a "whistleing swan," thus distinguishing it from the "large swan" (trumpeter swan) they had seen earlier on the Great Plains. Lewis thus should be given credit for discovering and first describing the trumpeter swan. Trumpeter swan populations have been recovering in North

Fig. 19. Trumpeter swan, adult

America as a result of intensive management, and they are no longer on the federal list of endangered species.

Western Meadowlark *Sturnella neglecta* FIG. 20

This bird, later described by Audubon as a new species, was almost certainly what Captain Clark observed in large numbers on the plains around Spirit Mound, now Clay County, near Vermillion, South Dakota, on August 25, 1804. He said the species was about the size of a "partridge" but with a short tail. Captain Lewis later gave an accurate description of a western meadowlark seen near Great Falls, Montana, on June 22, 1805. He contrasted it with the "old field

Fig. 20. Western meadowlark, adult male

lark" (eastern meadowlark, *Sturnella magna*) of the Atlantic states, noting the two species' considerable differences in vocalizations and their slight differences in other attributes. The vocal differences noted by Lewis are the most significant distinctions between these two species, and were also mentioned by Audubon when he later described and painted the western meadowlark. Western meadowlarks were also reported near Missoula on July 2, 1806. Their populations have decreased significantly in North America during the last four decades, reflecting losses in grassland habitats.

## (Western Tanager  *Piranga ludoviciana*)

This species was not mentioned in the expedition journals, but Wilson (*American Ornithology*) concluded from information reported to him by expedition members that western tanagers "inhabit the extensive plains or prairies of the Missouri, between the Osage and Mandan nations; building their nests in low grass." This must have been a mistaken attribution by Wilson, as neither the habitat nor the nest site fits the ecology of this western forest-dwelling songbird.

Fig. 21. Whooping crane, adult

## Whooping Crane *Grus americana* FIG. 21

Near the future site of Fort Berthold, North Dakota, some "large white cranes" were seen passing up the Missouri River on April 11, 1805. They were accurately described as being entirely white except for the larger wing feathers. These currently extremely rare and nationally endangered birds were also reported from western Oregon by Captain Clark, but there is no other evidence that whooping cranes ever occurred that far west, and so this identification seems questionable.

### Plants

## Aromatic (Fragrant) Sumac (Squaw bush)
### *Rhus aromatica,* var. *trilobata*

This is a widespread aromatic shrub whose edible fruits were used as food and for medicinal purposes and teas. The leaves are rich in tannins, and leaf or root extracts were widely used by Native Americans to stop bleeding and for treating a variety of other ailments. Dried leaves often comprised parts of smoking mixtures, which among the Omahas might also contain dogwood (*Cornus*) bark and Indian tobacco. The flexible green shoots were used for basket-making, and the roots were a source of yellow dye. Collected October 1, 1804, in present-day Stanley County, South Dakota, near the Cheyenne River.

### Aromatic Aster  *Aster oblongifolius*

This is a widespread native perennial forb. A related species, *Aster novae-angliae*, was an important medicinal plant for Native Americans, used both externally and internally in the form of teas. Smoke produced from burning it was also believed to help revive an unconscious person. Collected September 21, 1804, in present-day Lyman County, South Dakota, in the Big Bend region.

### Bearberry (Kinnikinnick)  *Arctostaphylos uva-ursi*  FIG. 22

A widespread evergreen shrub of the northern plains and woodlands. The fruits of this species were sometimes cooked and eaten. Its dried leaves were smoked as a substitute for tobacco by many northern tribes of Native Americans, or were mixed in with dogwood bark, tobacco, or other smoking materials. Its Native American name *kinnikinnick* is from the Algonquian language, probably meaning "a mixture" or "one who mixes," attesting to its widespread use for smoking by Native Americans. Collected during the winter of 1804–5 in present-day McLean County, North Dakota, probably at Fort Mandan.

### Broom Snakeweed (Broomweed)  *Gutierrezia sarothrae*

A widespread perennial forb. The stems of this species were often used by Native Americans for making brooms, and various parts of the plant were chewed and placed on insect stings or other venomous bites. Its use in treating snakebite is the basis for its vernacular name. The Lakotas boiled the plant to make a tea to treat dizziness and respiratory problems. Collected September 19, 1804, probably in present-day Buffalo County, South Dakota, in the Big Bend region. A newly discovered species.

### Canada Milk-vetch  *Astragalus canadensis*

This is a widespread perennial legume that, unlike many other species of *Astragalus*, is nonpoisonous. The Omaha–Ponca tribe used the dried pods as rattles; the Lakotas chewed the roots to relieve chest pains and made a root decoction to treat fever in children. Collected September 15, 1804, probably in present-day Brule County, South Dakota.

### Creeping Juniper (Shrubby Red Cedar)  *Juniperus horizontalis*

This is a widespread, prostrate evergreen shrub whose cones were used by plains natives to make tea for treating kidney problems. Like the other junipers, its leaves are high in volatile oils. Its fruit is often eaten by birds, which helps

Fig. 22. Bearberry

spread the seeds. Collected October 16, 1804, probably in present-day Emmons County, North Dakota. A newly discovered species.

## Dwarf (Common) Juniper *Juniperus communis*

This is a shrubby evergreen tree that, like all junipers, had many uses by Native Americans, including purification rites and other rituals, as well as for cures. Omaha creation myths associated the juniper with thunder, thunderbirds, or human origins. The twigs possess a strong diuretic component and a volatile oil comprised of monoterpenes. The berrylike fruits were eaten, used as flavorings, or boiled for tea. They are still used as flavoring in gin and in other alcoholic as well as nonalcoholic beverages. Collected October 17, 1804, probably in present-day Sioux County, North Dakota.

### Dwarf (Silver or Hoary) Sagebrush  *Artemisia cana*

This is a widespread perennial and aromatic shrub that was used by Native Americans for varied medicinal purposes, such as a cough medicine. Lakota men also made bracelets with it for use during the extremely painful sun dance, and both men and women used it to ward off evil influences by burning the plant or drinking tea made from it. Collected October 1 and 2, 1804, probably in present-day Stanley County, South Dakota, near the Cheyenne River, and also the following day, near the Sully-Porter county line. A newly discovered species.

### False Indigo  *Amorpha fruticosa*

The leaves of this perennial leguminous shrub and other species of *Amorpha* were used by Native Americans for smoking, making tea, and for medicinal purposes, such as a vermifuge. This plant and the related leadplant (*Amorpha canescens*) contain cannabinoid substances that might help account for their use in medicines. Collected August 27, 1806, in present-day Lyman or Buffalo County, South Dakota, in the Big Bend region. A newly discovered species.

### Fire-on-the-Mountain  *Euphorbia cyathophora*

This is a perennial forb that, like other species of its genus, accumulates potent alkaloids in its leaves and elsewhere. The milky sap also contains a variety of toxic diterpenes. Nevertheless, some species of *Euphorbia* were used by Native Americans for making medicinal teas, these probably serving as purges or emetics. Collected October 15, 1804, probably in present-day Sioux County, North Dakota.

### Fringed (White) Sagebrush  *Artemisia ludoviciana*  FIG. 23

A widespread aromatic subshrub of the arid West that was used by some Native American tribes for varied male ceremonial purposes (thus it was sometimes called "man sage"). It was also used as a medicine for diverse ills, for padding in pillows and saddle pads, and the dried plants were burned to help drive away mosquitoes. Collected October 1, 1804, in present-day Dewey, Sully, or Stanley County, South Dakota, or possibly on April 10, 1806, in present-day Washington or Oregon.

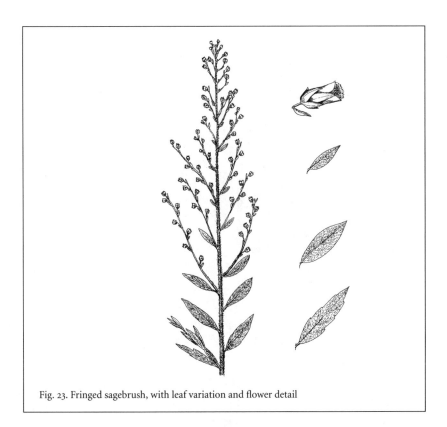

Fig. 23. Fringed sagebrush, with leaf variation and flower detail

## Indian ("Rikara") Tobacco  *Nicotiana quadrivalvus*  FIG. 24

This non-native forb is a species of tobacco that grows wild from Oregon to California and Nevada, but it evidently migrated east through cultivation by Native Americans, who grew it for smoking. It was cultivated by all the tribes of the Missouri Valley and was greatly favored over the related tobacco species *N. rustica*, which was widely used by Native peoples from the Mississippi River eastward. All the parts of the plant were dried and smoked, but the dried seed capsules were most prized. The plant matures in 60 to 65 days, and it continues to bear fruit until frost. Collected October 12, 1804, at an Arikara village near the present-day Walworth-Campbell county line, South Dakota. A newly discovered species.

## Lanceleaf Sage  *Salvia reflexa* (= "*lanceolata*")  FIG. 25

This is a widespread perennial forb. Its possible use by Native Americans is not clear, but many sages of this genus (not *Artemisia*) have long been used for

Fig. 24. Indian tobacco

cooking spices or as herbal teas. Collected September 21, 1804, in present-day Lyman County, South Dakota. A newly discovered species.

### Large-flowered Clammyweed  *Polanisia dodecandra trachysperma*
FIG. 26

This annual weedy forb was reportedly collected on August 25, presumably in 1804, when the expedition was in the vicinity of Vermillion (Clay County), South Dakota. The plant is widespread on the Great Plains and is a close relative of Rocky Mountain beeplant. (For its possible medicinal uses by Native Americans, see the entry for Rocky Mountain beeplant in the previous chapter).

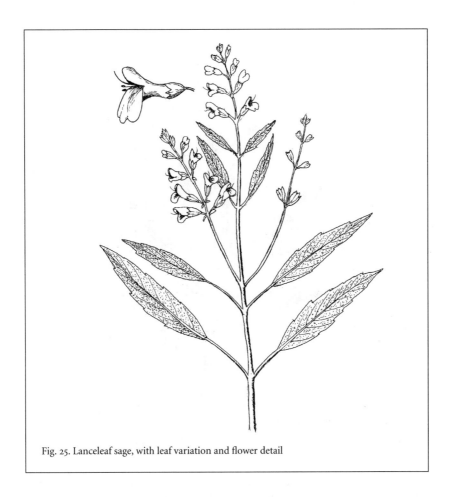

Fig. 25. Lanceleaf sage, with leaf variation and flower detail

## Long-leaved Sagebrush (Mugwort) *Artemisia longifolia*

This is a widespread, arid-adapted and aromatic subshrub that, like other species of *Artemisia,* is aromatic and was similarly used for medicinal purposes. The chewed root was used by men of the Omahas and Winnebagos as a love-charm, by spreading it on their clothing. The Pawnees used a decoction made from these plants for bathing and as a rheumatism treatment. Collected October 3, 1804, in present-day Porter or Sully County, South Dakota, near the Cheyenne River.

## Missouri Milk-vetch *Astragalus missouriensis* FIG. 27

This is a widespread perennial legume that, like Canada milk-vetch, is also nonpoisonous. Possible Native American use is not clear, but many of the *Astra-*

Fig. 26. Large-flowered clammyweed, with flower detail

*galus* species (especially the locoweeds) are known to have significant adverse physiological effects as a result of toxic alkaloids and/or selenium accumulations. Collected September 18, 1804, in present-day Brule County, South Dakota, near Chamberlain.

### Pin (Bird) Cherry  *Prunus pennsylvanica*

This cherry was the last plant specimen collected by Captain Lewis, on August 10, 1806, in western North Dakota, and was described in some detail by him on August 12, while he was being treated for a gunshot wound. It has at times been identified as *Prunus virginiana.*

### Purple Coneflower  *Echinacea angustifolia*

Although not represented in the herbarium specimens, seeds of what was probably this species were sent to President Jefferson by Captain Lewis, with

Fig. 27. Missouri milk-vetch

a comment that this plant is a valuable remedy for snakebite. Nearly all Great Plains tribes used this species medicinally, primarily using macerations of the root, or drinking a tea made from the root as a general painkiller and especially for snakebites. Recent work indicates that oils and polysaccharides are present in the root which have antibiotic, immunostimulatory, and even insecticidal qualities.

Rabbitbrush  *Chrysothamnus nauseosus*
(now *Ericameria nauseosa*)

This widespread perennial shrub of sagelands and shortgrass prairies produces a gummy secretion used for making tea, as a cough syrup, and for chest pains. The dried yellow flowers were also a source of a dye pigment. Collected October 1804, possibly in present-day Dewey or Sully County, South Dakota.

### Rough Gayfeather (Large Button Snakeroot) *Liatris aspera*

This widespread perennial forb belongs to a genus often used as medicines by many Native American tribes of the Great Plains. The edible roots were sometimes eaten but were more often used as treatments for a wide array of ailments. Thus, the Pawnees boiled the enlarged root and ate it to treat diarrhea, and the ground flower heads were mixed with corn and fed to horses to increase their endurance. The physiologic basis for these varied medicinal applications is not known, but the traditional use of the root for treating snakebite is the basis for the vernacular English name snakeroot. Collected September 12, 1804, in present-day Brule County, South Dakota.

### Shadscale (Bushy Atriplex, Four-wing Saltbush)
*Atriplex canescens* FIG. 28

The abundant seeds of this widespread perennial and alkali-tolerant shrub were ground up and used for bread flour. Collected September 21, 1804, in present-day Lyman County, South Dakota, in the Big Bend region. A newly discovered species.

### Silky Wormwood (False Tarragon or Linear-leaved Wormwood)
*Artemisia dracunculus* FIG. 29

This is a widespread perennial and aromatic forb that also occurs in Eurasia. It was used by the Pawnees for treating rheumatism, and its dried stems were used as brooms. All sage species probably contain artemisin and santonin, both lactone glycosides that have vermifuge properties, thus the name "wormwood" has been applied to some species. A terpenelike essential oil, thujone, is also present and may help account for the medicinal effects of sages. Collected September 15, 1804, in present-day Lyman or Brule County, South Dakota, near Chamberlain.

### Silver-leaf Scurfpea *Psoralea (Pediomelum) argophylla*

This is a widespread perennial legume. The seeds are poisonous to humans, but the plant is grazed to a slight extent by pronghorns and deer. The Santee Sioux used a decoction for treating horse wounds, and many plains tribes made a tea from its leaves for treating constipation. The ground-up foliage was also mixed with grease and rubbed on the body to treat fever. Collected October 17, 1804, probably in present-day Sioux County, North Dakota, near the Cannonball River. A newly discovered species.

Fig. 28. Shadscale, with seed detail

Spiny Goldenweed (Cutleaf Ironplant or Sideranthus)
*Machaeranthera pinnatifida (Haplopappus spinulosus)*
    This is a widespread and hardy perennial forb that is highly drought-resistant.
Because of its spiny leaves, it is grazed very little by wildlife, and its possible use
by Native Americans is unknown. Collected September 15, 1804, in present-day
Lyman or Brule County, South Dakota, near Chamberlain. A newly discovered
species.

Thick-spike Gayfeather (Prairie Button Snakeroot)
*Liatris pycnostachya*
    This is a widespread perennial forb that was eaten and used for medicine by
Native Americans. Collected September 15, 1804, probably in present-day Brule
County, South Dakota.

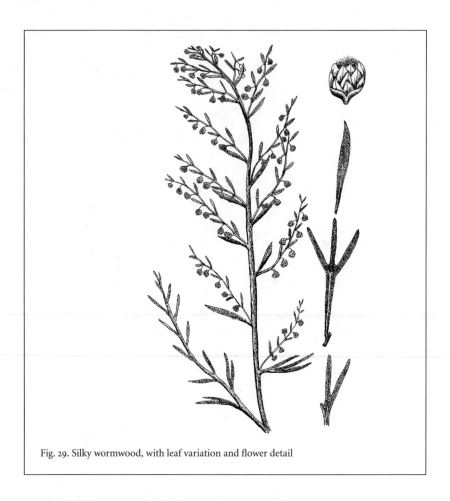

Fig. 29. Silky wormwood, with leaf variation and flower detail

## Western Red Cedar (Rocky Mountain Juniper)
### *Juniperus scopulorum* FIG. 30

A widespread evergreen shrub or small tree. Many western tribes made teas from juniper roots or leaves, or smoked the green twigs, probably for their terpenelike oils. The fruits were eaten raw or cooked, used as flavorings, or ground up and used in cooking. A wax extracted from the berries was also used for making candles. Collected October 2, 1804, probably in present-day Sully or Porter County, South Dakota.

## White Milkwort *Polygala alba*

This is a widespread perennial forb widely used by Native Americans for medicinal purposes. For example, the Santee Sioux used it for earaches. A closely

Fig. 30. Western juniper and adult lark sparrow

related species, *P. senega*, was used by Native Americans as an antidote for many kinds of poisoning, including snakebites. Collected August 10, 1806, probably in present-day McKenzie County, North Dakota. A newly discovered species.

### Wild Alfalfa (Few-flowered Psoralea)  *Psoralidium (Psoralea) tenuiflora*

This is a widespread perennial legume. Native Americans made a tea of the stems and leaves as a cure for fever; tea made from the roots was used for treating headaches. The Lakotas burned the roots as a mosquito repellant, and the Santee Sioux boiled the roots to form part of a tuberculosis medicine. *Psoralea* species produce a substance (psoralin) still under investigation for possible use in several diseases, including immune-system diseases. Collected September 21, 1804, in present-day Lyman County, South Dakota, in the Big Bend region. A newly discovered species.

The closely related breadroot scurfpea (*Psoralea esculenta*), also called Indian breadfruit or prairie turnip, is widespread in the northern Great Plains and has been described by Kelly Kindscher as "the most important wild food of the Plains Indians." Its root was used by the Blackfoot for making medicinal tea or directly chewed for various ailments. A specimen was collected during the expedition, but the date and location of its collection are questionable. Thus it is given uncertain placement here.

# Montana

## Summary of Route and Major Biological Discoveries

On April 27, 1805, the expedition left the mouth of the Yellowstone River and probably passed the boundary of present-day Montana that same day. The courses of the Yellowstone and Missouri Rivers have changed greatly in the past two centuries, leaving room for some doubt as to the exact day the party reached what is now the eastern border of Montana. They very soon encountered large numbers of deer, elk, bison, wolves, and grizzly bears. They reached "Martha's River" (now the Big Muddy River) on April 29 and the "Porcupine River" (now the Poplar River) on May 3. The Milk River was reached on May 8 and the Musselshell on May 20. "Judith's River" (now the Judith River) was passed on May 29 and the mouth of "Maria's River" (now simply spelled the Marias River) on June 2, 1805.

A major geographic discovery, the Great Falls of the Missouri River, was reached on June 16, 1805. At that point a major portage was needed, and it was not until July 15 that the party was able to get under way again. Captain Clark and his small advance party reached the Three Forks region on July 25, where the Jefferson, Madison, and Gallatin Rivers (all named by Lewis and Clark) merge to form the Missouri. It was also near here that Sacagawea had been captured five years previously. At Three Forks the expedition had reached an elevation of slightly more than 4,000 feet and was at the very western edge of the Great Plains. The rest of the group arrived the 17th, and after three more days of local exploration they set off again. Following the westernmost branch (Jefferson River) upstream, the expedition soon was in the heart of the Rocky Mountains and about to cross the Continental Divide.

The route of the return trip across Montana is complicated by the fact that the expedition split into several parties after crossing the Rocky Mountains at Lolo Pass, west of present-day Missoula. From Travelers' Rest camp (about 20 miles south of Missoula) Captain Clark and a group of 20 men, plus Sacagawea and her son, began traveling southward on July 3, progressively making their

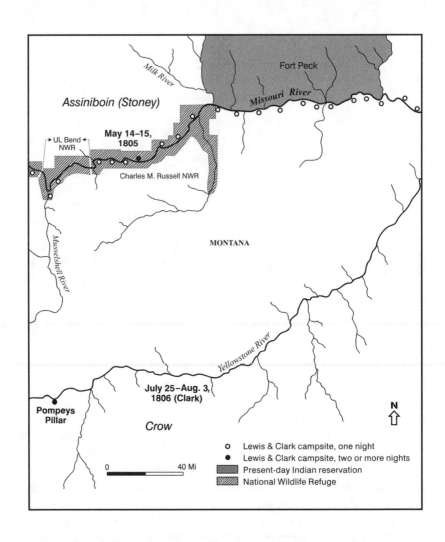

Map 5. Route of Lewis and Clark in Eastern Montana

OUTWARD ROUTE SCHEDULE: April 27 to July 27, 1805

RETURN SCHEDULE: July 7 to August 3 (Clark) or August 7 (Lewis), 1806

RIVER DISTANCE: Montana–North Dakota border to Three Forks, 945 river miles, according to Lewis and Clark. Because of recent impoundments, present-day river distances are now substantially less than the original distances calculated by Lewis and Clark.

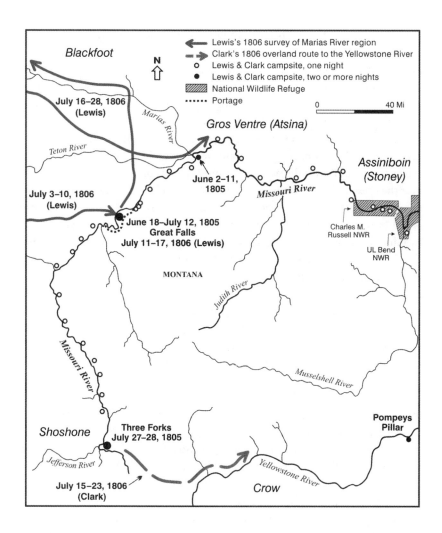

Map 6. Route of Lewis and Clark in Western Montana as Far as Three Forks

OUTWARD ROUTE SCHEDULE: April 27 to July 27, 1805

RETURN SCHEDULE: July 7 to August 3 (Clark) and August 7 (Lewis), 1806

RIVER DISTANCE: Montana–North Dakota border to Three Forks, 945 river miles, according to Lewis and Clark. Because of recent impoundments, present-day river distances are now substantially less than the original distances calculated by Lewis and Clark.

way past the sites of present-day Hamilton and Jackson. On July 8 they reached the Beaverhead River somewhat above the location of present-day Dillon, where they found their cache of supplies as well as their canoes. From there they moved downstream to Three Forks, arriving July 13, 1806. Ten members of Captain Clark's group were then sent via canoes from Three Forks to Great Falls, to begin the arduous portage around the falls and rapids.

Captain Clark and his remaining 12-person contingent (10 men plus Sacagawea and her 17-month-old son, Baptiste) and their horses moved overland across Bozeman Pass and reached the upper Yellowstone ("Rochejhone") River near the present site of Livingston on July 15, 1806. There the trees were not large enough to make canoes, so they continued downstream. At the approximate site of present-day Columbus the group stopped long enough to manufacture two dugout canoes from cottonwoods and then resumed water travel on July 24. They gradually made their way down the Yellowstone, making a short stop on July 25 at a sandstone promontory that Clark named "Pompy's Tower" in honor of Sacagawea's son, whom Clark had nicknamed Pompy. There Captain Clark inscribed his own name and the date. In that general vicinity they saw a large herd of bighorns as well as flocks of geese and pigeons. They arrived at the mouth of the Yellowstone on August 3, 1806, thus finally leaving present-day eastern Montana and again passing into what is now western North Dakota.

From Travelers' Rest camp, Captain Lewis and his group of nine men (and five guides) independently set forth in a northeasterly direction on July 3, 1806, for Great Falls, arriving at the river after a hard march of eight days. He left six of his party at Great Falls to assist Clark's ten-man contingent with the downstream portaging, and with his remaining three handpicked men headed on July 16 for a brief reconnaissance of the Marias ("Maria's") River. On their way north, they sequentially crossed the Sun River ("Medicine River") and the Teton River. After reaching the Marias, Lewis doggedly followed it northwest to a point about 20 miles west of present-day Cut Bank, along a northern tributary, Cut Bank Creek. He was searching for the northernmost limits of the Missouri's drainage, and thus the possible northernmost legal limits of the Louisiana Purchase. By July 22 he was within sight of the Rocky Mountains, but the river had still not turned north, and several days of bad weather had made it impossible for him to establish his exact location. After turning back south and crossing Two Medicine River (the south fork of Maria's River in Lewis's terminology), the exploration ended abruptly on July 27 when eight Piegan Blackfoot men, with whom they had held a peaceful council the day before, tried to steal the group's guns and horses. In the resulting fight one Blackfoot man was killed and another was evidently fatally wounded. Lewis himself was very narrowly missed by a musket ball. Lewis and his men quickly retreated and again reached the Missouri River near the present site of Virgelle on July 28. The site of this harrowing encounter is on private land about 15 miles northeast of present-day Valier.

The group of six men who had been left by Captain Lewis to negotiate the Great Falls portage was soon met by the ten others who had been sent downstream by Captain Clark from Three Forks to help with the portaging. After negotiating the Great Falls portage, the 16 men continued downstream. By the greatest of good luck, they encountered Lewis and his three-man party just as they were returning to the mouth of the Marias River on July 28. The reunited group of 20 men then descended the Missouri under the leadership of Captain Lewis, reaching the mouth of the Yellowstone River and arriving at the approximate present-day boundary of North Dakota on August 7, 1806, only four days behind Captain Clark's group that had come via the Yellowstone. Thus the last members of the Corps of Discovery departed from what is now Montana.

# Mammals

### Bighorn Sheep  *Ovis canadensis auduboni*

In Montana, bighorns were reported from at least 15 locations, and at least 35 were killed during the entire expedition. As noted previously, bighorn sheep were first observed at the mouth of the Yellowstone River in extreme western North Dakota and were subsequently seen as far west as the Beaverhead Mountains in Montana. In one location below the mouth of the Marias River the party killed nine sheep in a single day. None was seen along the upper Marias River by Captain Lewis. The bighorn was formally described and named in 1804. The species still ranges widely in the American and Canadian Rocky Mountains, and the poorly characterized race *O. c. auduboni* historically inhabited the upper Great Plains from Nebraska to North Dakota at the time of the Lewis and Clark expedition. It was first distinguished subspecifically from the more widespread Rocky Mountain form in 1901. The last state record for native bighorns in North Dakota was in 1905, for South Dakota in about 1915, and for Nebraska in 1918. Reintroduced bighorns of the nearly identical Rocky Mountain race now occur in Nebraska's Pine Ridge and Wildcat Hills, in South Dakota's Black Hills and Badlands National Park, and in North Dakota's Theodore Roosevelt National Park.

### Bison  *Bison bison*

Bison were reported in present-day Montana from at least 33 locations, from the North Dakota boundary west up the Missouri Valley almost to Great Falls, along the Sun and Marias Rivers, and along the Yellowstone Valley from about present-day Billings to the North Dakota boundary. After the great bison slaughter of the middle and late nineteenth century, when more than 40 million animals were destroyed, the only remaining bison south of Canada were a few hundred individuals that were protected in Yellowstone National Park. From these and from some small captive herds the present population of several hundred thousand bison has been produced.

### Bushy-tailed Woodrat  *Neotoma cinerea*  FIG. 31

The bushy-tailed woodrat was first accurately described by Lewis and Clark, but the species was not formally named until 1815. They encountered it in the vicinity of Great Falls on July 2, 1805, and captured a live specimen. Captain Lewis described it with care, noting that he had often seen the animals' dens in cliff and tree hollows, and that they often eat the fruits and seeds of the prickly pear (*Opuntia* sp.). Woodrats, more generally known as "packrats," accumulate caches of food items such as cactus fruits, acorns, pine cones, bones, and even

Fig. 31. Bushy-tailed woodrat, adult with cache

inedible objects such as small plastic items and other miscellaneous "treasures" that they happen to find in the vicinities of their nests. It is now known that bushy-tailed woodrats extend east into the western Dakotas, and a few decades after Lewis and Clark's expedition Prince Maximilian found them to be present at both Fort Clark and Fort Union.

## (Columbian Ground Squirrel *Spermophilus columbianus*)

Lewis and Clark made many observations of the Columbian ground squirrel on the western slope of the Rockies, but only a few apply to the extreme western Great Plains. In July of 1806 Clark encountered this species in the upper Bitterroot Valley, and during Lewis's independent survey of the Marias River region during the same month he encountered these animals east of present-day Missoula and on the Cut Bank branch of the Marias River. The Columbian ground squirrel was first described by Lewis and Clark on the basis of specimens they obtained in Oregon, but it was not given a formal Latin name until 1815. This species is primarily associated geographically with the Columbia River Basin much farther to the west.

## Coyote  *Canis latrans*

At a minimum, coyotes were encountered near Wolf Point and on the upper Marias River in Montana, but they were evidently much less common than gray wolves there and were only rarely mentioned. They became much more common everywhere after the disappearance of gray wolves from the Great Plains, and have gradually extended their range eastward to the Atlantic coast. In spite of massive poisoning and other control efforts, the coyote has thrived better than any other native American dog or cat.

## Elk  *Cervus elaphus*

In Montana, elk were reported from at least 37 locations, from around the present-day North Dakota boundary west along the Missouri Valley to its Three Forks headwaters, in the mountains to the Bitterroot Valley, and along the entire Yellowstone Valley. They were also seen along the Sun River and in the Marias River valley near present-day Shelby. They were especially numerous along the Yellowstone River, where herds of up to 200 were apparently common. They are still locally common in Montana but are mainly confined to forested areas and sanctuaries. Elk were eliminated from Nebraska and North Dakota by the early 1880s and from South Dakota by 1888. Restoration efforts have occurred in all three states, and small, mostly confined herds exist in them.

## Gray Wolf  *Canis lupus*

Wolves were especially common in Montana, where they were reported from at least 17 locations, and the herds of bison were regularly "attended by their shepherds the wolves." Near the mouth of the Sun ("Medicine") River Captain Lewis noted that most of the wolves seen around a bison carcass "were of the large kind." Gray wolves were eventually extirpated from Montana, but recent releases in the Yellowstone Park area have restored them to the state's faunal list. They have since been seen as far south and east as Wyoming's Wind River Range.

## Grizzly Bear  *Ursus arctos*

During the 1805 ascent up the Missouri grizzlies were seen by expedition members at no fewer than 17 locations, and Lewis also mentioned them at three locations during his survey of the Marias River valley. Clark likewise saw them at least twice as he traveled down the Yellowstone Valley. Lewis and Clark referred to grizzly bears under various names, including the "white bear," "brown bear," and "grizly bear." Captain Lewis eventually concluded that all these color variants were "of the same species only differing in color from age or more properly from the same natural cause than many other anamals of the same family differ in coulur." The grizzly bear was not formally described and named as a distinct species ("*Ursus ferox*") until 1815, based on the descriptions and specimens of Lewis and Clark. Raymond Burroughs calculated that at least 43 grizzly bears were killed over the entire expedition period, most of them in Montana. Twenty three were killed between the mouth of the Yellowstone and Three Forks, Montana. Ten were killed in the vicinity of Great Falls alone, and 14 were killed during the separate return trips of Lewis and Clark down the Yellowstone and Missouri Rivers of Montana. Every shooting of a grizzly was a highly risky undertaking. One enormous 600-pound male required ten shots to bring it down. On May 14 six men set out to kill a grizzly bear. Although all six lead balls hit the bear, it attacked, and only after two more bullets struck it, one in the head, did it finally collapse, just before reaching its closest human target. Montana now has one of the very few remaining populations of grizzly bears south of Canada, with perhaps 500 to 1,000 surviving in the northern Rockies of the United States and Canada, centering on the Glacier-Banff-Jasper ecosystem. There are a few left in the Yellowstone Park ecosystem, and they range east and south locally to Wyoming's Wind River Range.

## (Moose  *Alces alces*)

Several "moose deer" were reportedly seen on May 10, 1805, in present-day Dawson County, Montana, according to Sergeant Ordway's journal. No other information was provided, and the identification seems rather unlikely, given this geographic location in the high plains of eastern Montana, well away from typical moose habitat.

## Mountain Lion  *Puma concolor*

A few encounters with mountain lions occurred while the expedition was still on the Great Plains. On May 16, between the Milk and Musselshell Rivers, a mountain lion ("panther") was shot and wounded, but it escaped. One was killed on the Jefferson River on August 3, 1805, and a few days later three deer-skins disappeared from camp and were judged to have been stolen by a mountain lion. In spite of continuous persecution ever since, mountain lions have somehow survived in the Rocky Mountains and Black Hills regions. Occasionally stray animals still wander east into Nebraska and eastern South Dakota and North Dakota, usually with fatal results to the cats. Their prime prey, mule deer and white-tailed deer, have vastly increased in the absence of large predators such as wolves and mountain lions, but the increased human population has had little tolerance for mountain lions, and most that stray into the Great Plains are quickly killed.

## Mule Deer *Odocoileus hemionus*
## and White-tailed Deer *Odocoileus virginianus*

Deer of unspecified species were reported by Lewis and Clark from at least 33 Montana locations, in addition to nine reports specifically of mule deer and two of white-tailed deer. White-tailed deer were seen west along the Missouri River to about Wolf Point, and mule deer from that point west up the Missouri Valley to the Rocky Mountains. In recent years white-tailed deer have been increasing relative to mule deer in the western Great Plains and are now as common as mule deer at least as far west as western North Dakota and western Nebraska.

## Northern Pocket Gopher *Thomomys talpoides*

Although Lewis and Clark did not actually observe these reclusive animals, Captain Lewis described their characteristic tunnels and mounds, so to a limited degree he may be credited with discovering the species. The northern pocket gopher was not formally named until 1828.

## Northern River Otter *Lontra canadensis*

In Montana, otters were reported by Lewis and Clark from at least 15 locations; they were especially numerous between Great Falls and the vicinity of Three Forks, where water clarity and associated fishing opportunities were certainly better than were typical farther downstream. At the time of the Lewis and Clark expedition otter pelts were not nearly as highly valued as beaver pelts, and little attention was paid to them. However, Native Americans prized their fur, which was used for ceremonial paraphernalia. Medicine sacks were also made from their skins.

## Pronghorn *Antilocapra americana*

Pronghorns were reported from at least 47 Montana locations, from approximately the North Dakota boundary up the Missouri Valley to a point beyond present-day Dillon, in the Sun and Marias Valleys, and down the Yellowstone Valley from present-day Livingston to the mouth of the Bighorn River.

## Red Fox *Vulpes vulpes*

In Montana, red foxes were reported from at least three locations, as compared with only one coyote reference and 17 locations where wolves were mentioned. Red foxes and swift foxes have both generally suffered in recent decades, inasmuch as these small foxes are regularly killed by coyotes. Coyotes have increased in the Great Plains because their populations are no longer being controlled by gray wolves.

## Swift Fox  *Vulpes velox*  FIG. 32

The swift fox was first recognized as a distinct species by Lewis and Clark but was not formally described and scientifically named until 1823. It was first encountered on July 6, 1805, in the vicinity of Great Falls. At that time Captain Lewis referred to the animal as a "remarkable small fox." Two days later one was shot, and it was carefully described by Lewis. He noted its remarkably long claws, and later (July 26) mentioned the black tip of its tail, another distinguishing features of the species. This high plains species is now barely surviving in Nebraska, the Dakotas, and eastern Montana, with very few recent records for any of these states. There are only two North Dakota records since 1976 (Mercer and Golden Valley Counties), and four southwestern South Dakota counties have recent records. There may also be some swift foxes left in the nearby Oglala National Grassland of northwestern Nebraska and in Nebraska's Box Butte County, where some were photographed in 2001. Perhaps some also survive in the extreme southwestern counties of Nebraska near the Pawnee National Grassland of adjacent Colorado, where they are known to occur. Swift foxes are easily trapped, and in most areas have lost prairie dogs as part of their food base.

## Thirteen-lined Ground Squirrel  *Spermophilus tridecemlineatus*  
FIG. 33

This common ground squirrel of the northern plains was not mentioned until the expedition had entered Montana, even through the species is extremely common in the Dakotas and Nebraska. It was first noted near the Great Falls on July 4, 1805, when Captain Lewis obtained a live specimen and carefully described it. The thirteen-lined ground squirrel was not formally described and named until 1821. It is still one of the most commonly seen and widespread rodents of the northern plains, and is a major food for coyotes, badgers, and other grassland predators. Like other ground squirrels, it is dormant for more than half of the year, which may reduce predation levels.

## Birds

## American Avocet  *Recurvirostra americana*

There is no doubt as to the identity of the bird shot on May 1, 1805, about 75 miles above the mouth of the Yellowstone River. It was carefully described by Captain Lewis, who incorrectly believed it new to science. He called it the "Missouri plover." Avocets are still fairly widespread in the more alkaline wetlands

Fig. 32. Swift fox, adult

of western North America; their uniquely recurved bills are mainly used for extracting small invertebrates from the surface of water by a kind of lateral scything action.

### American Goldfinch  *Carduelis tristis*

Lewis also mentions seeing goldfinches among the birds singing along the Marias River in Montana on June 8, 1805. He was apparently quite familiar with this widespread woodland-and-edge species and gave it no special attention. Goldfinch populations have declined significantly in the past four decades.

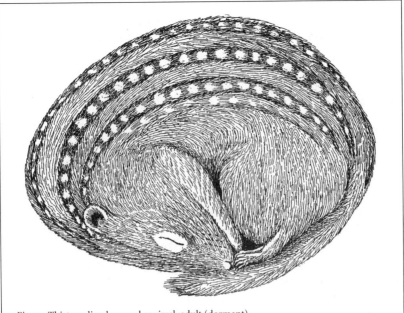

Fig. 33. Thirteen-lined ground squirrel, adult (dormant)

### Belted Kingfisher  *Ceryle alcyon*

In the expedition's Meteorological Register of May 23, 1805, it was noted that a kingfisher was first seen seasonally near present-day Fort Peck. It was also seen near Great Falls (July 11–13, 1805). This distinctive bird is still common along relatively clear rivers supporting small fishes. Belted kingfisher populations have declined significantly in North America during the last four decades, probably as a result of increased levels of water pollution.

### Brown-headed Cowbird  *Molothrus ater*
### and Brewer's Blackbird  *Euphagus cyanocephalus*

Few specific notes were made on these presumably common and probably widespread species, which are adapted to forage at the feet of large ungulates such as bison. In the expedition's Meteorological Register of May 17, 1805, it was noted that "large and small blackbirds" had returned to eastern Montana. Elliott Coues identified these as most probably brown-headed cowbirds and Brewer's blackbirds. Probable cowbirds were also seen near Great Falls (July 11–13, 1805, and July 11, 1806), and this species (referred to by the explorers as the "buffalo-pecker") must have regularly associated with bison before domestic cattle appeared on the Great Plains. Cowbird populations are now declining nationally, but they still pose a serious threat to native songbirds because of their parasitic nesting behavior. Brewer's blackbird populations have also declined significantly rangewide.

## Cliff Swallow  *Petrochelidon pyrrhonota*

On May 31, 1805, in what is now Chouteau County, Montana, Lewis saw a group of what he called "small martin" building globular nests of clay on a cliff wall. These could only have been cliff swallows, which now widely nest on vertical manmade structures, such as the sides of concrete bridges.

## Common Nighthawk  *Chordeiles minor*

On June 30, 1805, near Great Falls, Montana, Captain Lewis shot a bird he identified as a species of goatsucker, reporting that it was identical to those of the Atlantic states, "where it is called the large goat-sucker or night hawk." Nighthawks, whip-poor-wills, and poorwills are aerial insect-eaters; their extremely large mouths are responsible for their colorful if erroneous vernacular name "goatsuckers." Common nighthawk populations have declined significantly in North America during the last four decades, as have other goatsuckers.

## Eastern Kingbird  *Tyrannus tyrannus*
## or Western Kingbird  *Tyrannus verticalis*

Few specific notes were made on these rather conspicuous songbird species, and not enough information was offered to distinguish which kingbird species was seen. In the expedition's Meteorological Register of May 25, 1805, it was noted that the "king-bird or bee-martin" had returned seasonally to the vicinity of the mouth of the Musselshell River. Kingbirds are rather late spring arrivals in the northern United States, as they winter in tropical America. The eastern species is more likely to have been seen than the western, since the eastern would have been the one familiar to the explorers and would not have attracted special attention. Also, it is more often found closer to water than the more arid-adapted western species. Kingbirds of undetermined species were also noted on June 10, 1805, near the mouth of the Marias River, and on August 2, 1806, near present-day Missoula. The eastern kingbird's rangewide population has declined significantly during the past four decades.

## Greater Sage-grouse  *Centrocercus urophasianus*  FIG. 34

One of the species definitely discovered by Lewis and Clark is this large sage-adapted grouse. It was first seen on June 5, 1805, near the Marias River in Montana, when an attempt to kill one was unsuccessful. Others were seen at Lemhi

Pass in the Beaverhead Mountains on August 12 of that year, but it was not until October 17 that several were actually shot. Both Lewis and Clark provided detailed descriptions of the species, Clark calling it the "prarie cock" and Lewis the "cock of the plains." Lewis also first described the species' unusual saclike gizzard, describing it as more like a "maw" (crop) than a typical muscular grinding organ. He said this grouse feeds almost entirely on the "pulpy leafed thorn," presumably confusing the relatively inedible black greasewood with the bird's actual primary (almost sole) food, the highly nutritious leaves of big sagebrush (*Artemisia tridentata*). John J. Audubon used Lewis's' suggested name "cock of the plains" when he painted the species about three decades later. Greater sagegrouse populations have plummeted in recent decades, as the West's once-vast areas of native sagebrush have been progressively cleared.

## Lewis's Woodpecker  *Melanerpes lewis*  FIG. 35

One of the major ornithological discoveries of the expedition was Captain Lewis's discovery of the woodpecker that now bears his name. On July 20, 1805, along Prickly Pear Creek and near present-day Helena, Montana, Lewis first saw a "black woodpecker (or crow)." He judged it to be about the size of a flicker but as black as a crow. He was not able to obtain a specimen until May of 1806, when in Idaho the expedition members "killed and preserved several." He then provided a highly detailed description of the bird, and at least one of the preserved specimens made its way back east, where it eventually ended up in the hands of Charles W. Peale, curator of the Philadelphia Museum housed in Independence Hall. The specimen that Alexander Wilson used to illustrate the species for the first time was one of those collected by Lewis and Clark, and it was named "Lewis's woodpecker." Wilson's original sketches of this woodpecker and of Clark's nutcracker (*Nucifraga columbiana*), similarly named after Captain Clark, are still present in the Academy of Natural Sciences of Philadelphia. Like the red-headed woodpecker, the Lewis's woodpecker is distinctly migratory and often occurs well away from dense woods. Its population numbers have not changed significantly in the past four decades.

## Loggerhead Shrike  *Lanius ludovicianus*

Captain Lewis discovered the nest and eggs of the loggerhead shrike on June 10, 1805, near the mouth of the Marias River in Montana. He described it in considerable detail, thinking the species might be new to science. However, it later was recognized as an undescribed subspecies of an already known species. Lewis noted the shrike's hawklike claws and judged it to be a predator of insects. It is now known to prey also on a wide variety of animals, including both small mammals and birds. It is characteristic of open, often arid, country. Loggerhead

Fig. 34. Greater sage-grouse, adult male (right) and female

shrike populations have declined significantly in North America during the last four decades.

## Mallard  *Anas platyrhynchos*

Mallards, usually called "duckinmallards" by the explorers, were often seen but generally not distinguished from other duck species. However, they were mentioned specifically as present in the vicinity of Three Forks, Montana, on July 29, 1805, and again on August 2 on the Jefferson River above Three Forks. Mallard populations have probably increased substantially during the past century as a result of wildlife management programs.

## McCown's Longspur  *Calcarius mccownii*  FIG. 36

One June 4, 1805, near the mouth of the Marias River in Montana, Lewis saw a sparrow-sized bird taking flight, singing, and then dropping back to earth. His detailed description leaves little doubt that he had observed the McCown's

Fig. 35. Lewis's woodpecker, adult male (right) and female

longspur in its aerial territorial display. This species was not officially described and named until 1851, more than four decades later. It is a typical species of arid shortgrass prairies, and its population appears to be declining rangewide.

## Merganser  *Mergus* sp.

Lewis and Clark's "red-headed fishing duck" was judged by Elliott Coues to be the red-breasted merganser (*Mergus serrator*). This description applies only to female or immature male mergansers and would also fit the common merganser (*Mergus merganser*). Indeed, the common merganser is the typical breeding species of this region. Mergansers were observed on June 21, 1805, in the vicinity of Great Falls, as well as near the present-day locations of Helena (July 20, 1805), Townsend (July 24, 1805), and Whitehall (August 2, 1805). They are largely confined to fairly clear streams that permit visual hunting for fish, and common mergansers still breed locally in western Montana.

Fig. 36. McCown's longspur, adult male

## Mourning Dove  *Zenaida macroura*

Few specific notes were made on this common and well-known species. In the expedition's Meteorological Register of May 8, 1805, it was noted that the "turtle dove" had returned to northeastern Montana, near Fort Peck. It was seen near the mouth of the Marias River on June 8, 1805. On the return trip of 1806 it was observed near the present-day locations of Missoula and Billings, near Great Falls, and on the upper Marias River. Mourning dove populations have declined significantly in North America during the last four decades; they are a highly adaptable but heavily hunted species.

## Osprey  *Pandion haliaetus*

The "white-headed fishing hawk" was seen by Captain Lewis on August 9, 1805, near present-day Grayling, Montana. Lewis also noted that it had not been seen below the mouth of the Yellowstone River. He was clearly already familiar with this wide-ranging and fish-eating species, which favors hunting in clear water. Its population trends have been volatile, as like the bald eagle and other fish-eating birds it was seriously affected by pesticide poisoning during the mid–twentieth century.

(Pine Siskin *Carduelis pinus*)

Captain Lewis mentioned seeing the "linnet" on the Marias River on June 8, 1805, a bird name that has sometimes been associated with the pine siskin. However, several other small finches have historically been called linnets, and Lewis's identification seems rather unlikely given the location and date.

## Red-headed Woodpecker *Melanerpes erythrocephalus*

Few notes were made on this common and widespread species. In the expedition's Meteorological Register of May 28, 1805, it was noted that a "small black and white woodpecker with a red head, the same which is common in the Atlantic States" was seen in northern Montana near the mouth of the Judith River. It was also seen July 16, 1806, near Great Falls and near present-day Fort Peck on August 3, 1806. Unlike some similar-sized woodpeckers such as the downy and hairy, this is a seasonally migratory species, at least in the northern states. Its rangewide population has declined significantly in the past four decades.

## Sandhill Crane *Grus canadensis*

The first mention of sandhill cranes by Lewis came on July 15, 1805, in the vicinity of the Gates of the Rocky Mountains, Montana, where several examples of the "large brown or Sandhill crain" were seen leading young. A living young bird was also brought into camp on July 19, 1805, near Three Forks, Montana. Lewis eventually released it. Greater sandhill cranes (*Grus canadensis tabida*) continue to survive in the northern Rocky Mountain region and have been increasing both regionally and nationally in recent decades as a result of long-term protection.

## Upland Sandpiper *Bartramia longicauda*
## or Mountain Plover *Charadrius montanus*

On July 22, 1805, Captain Lewis reported seeing "a species of small curlooe of a brown color" at present-day Canyon Ferry, Montana. This bird was tentatively identified by Rueben Thwaites as a mountain plover, but Elliott Coues instead believed that it might have been an upland sandpiper. Either species would be geographically possible, but the sandpiper, which is somewhat more curlewlike than the plover and is more widespread, would seem the more likely possibility. Descriptive terms such as curlew (spelled variously) and plover were evidently used rather indiscriminately for shorebirds by expedition members, with curlew perhaps usually applied to the longer-billed or larger species. Too little information is available to make an informed guess as to the identity of this particular bird. The mountain plover's population has declined to the point that it is now a federally endangered species, whereas the population of the upland sandpiper has increased slightly during the past four decades, one of the very few grassland-adapted bird species that has shown this trend.

## Willet  *Catoptrophorus semipalmatus*

This species was collected on May 9, 1805, at the site of present-day Fort Peck, Montana. Captain Lewis described this bird with some care and detail, incorrectly thinking it might be new to science, and he especially noted its resemblance to the "large grey plover" or "Jack Curloo." He described the bird's wings as white, tipped with black, making identification of this distinctive species fairly certain. Like avocets, willets are still fairly common in the more alkaline wetlands of western North America.

## Reptiles

## (Painted turtle  *Chrysemys picta*)

"Water terrepens" were noted in the vicinity of Great Falls, Montana, on June 25, 1805. Their specific identity is in some doubt, but this might be a reference to the common and geographically widespread painted turtle.

## Prairie (Western) Rattlesnake  *Crotalus viridis*  FIG. 37

Many encounters with rattlesnakes were reported by the expedition; one of the earliest that certainly involved the prairie rattlesnake occurred May 17, 1805, near the mouth of the Yellowstone River. Rattlesnakes were also encountered in Missouri, Nebraska (in present-day Washington and Boyd Counties), and South Dakota (near the White River). Of these, the Missouri and southern Nebraska locations may possibly have involved the relatively large and more dangerous timber rattlesnakes (*Crotalus horridus*), but the later encounters on the high plains of the Dakotas and Montana most likely involved the somewhat smaller and then still-undescribed western or prairie rattler. Expedition members later encountered rattlesnakes at least a dozen times on the plains of Montana, including several near escapes from being bitten. The western rattlesnake was not formally described and given a Latin name until 1818.

## Softshell Turtle  *Apalone* sp.

Softshell turtles, probably representing the spiny softshell (*A. spinifera*), were mentioned as seen on the Missouri River of Montana above the mouth of the Musselshell River on May 26, 1805, and also on the Yellowstone River on July 19, 1806. These are fairly common river-dwelling turtles that were probably already well known to Captain Lewis and thus not considered worthy of special attention.

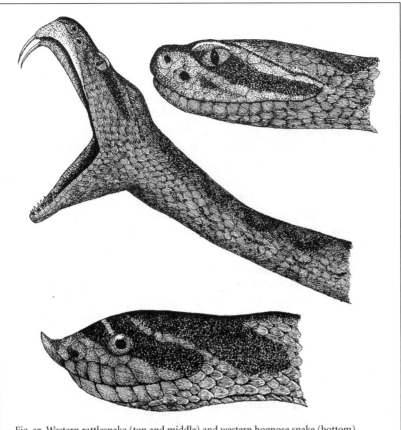

Fig. 37. Western rattlesnake (top and middle) and western hognose snake (bottom)

### Western (Wandering) Garter Snake  *Thamnophis elegans vagrans*

On July 24, 1804, Captain Lewis closely examined some snakes seen near Three Forks, Montana, and found them to be "much like the garter snake of our country." They have been tentatively identified by Elliott Coues as western garter snakes of the race *vagrans*.

### Western Hognose Snake  *Heterodon nasicus*  FIG. 37

A snake that Captain Lewis found and described on July 23, 1805, near present-day Townsend, Montana, most probably can be referred to this species. The western hognose snake was not formally described until 1852, so Lewis should be credited with discovering the species. It is mildly venomous and has a somewhat frightening, cobralike defensive display. Its distinctive upturned snout is used for digging in sand, where it searches for toads and other prey.

## Fish

### Channel Catfish *Ictalurus punctatus* and Blue Catfish *Ictalurus furcatus* FIG. 38

Catfish, most probably including both the channel and blue catfish, were caught and eaten at various points along the Missouri River, from Missouri to Montana. The channel catfish ranges upstream to Montana, and the blue catfish to the Dakotas. "White catfish" were caught in numbers, and one of the party's major Nebraska campsites (July 22–26, 1804, near present-day Lake Manawa) was named "White Catfish camp" because of the several large catfish caught there. Channel catfish and blue catfish both occur in this region and both closely resemble the white catfish (*Ictalurus catus*) of eastern North America. However, the blue catfish is on average considerably larger than the channel catfish, the largest known examples exceeding 100 pounds, whereas channel catfish rarely reach 30 pounds. Nine catfish caught near the mouth of the Vermillion River on August 25, 1804, collectively weighed nearly 300 pounds, which would strongly suggest that they were blue catfish.

### Cutthroat Trout *Salmo (Onchorhynchus) clarki* FIG. 38

This newly discovered species, later named in honor of Captain Clark, was first caught on June 13, 1805, in the vicinity of Great Falls. The species' detailed description by Captain Lewis leaves no doubt as to its identity.

### Goldeye *Hiodon alosoides* FIG. 39

Fish identified by Elliott Coues as goldeye, a previously unknown species, were caught on June 11, 1805, above the mouth of the Marias River. They were described by Captain Lewis as resembling the "hickory shad" (the gizzard shad, *Dorosoma*) or the "oldwife" (the alewife, *Alosa*), except for their large eyes and long teeth. The goldeye is predatory and does have unusually large, golden eyes and abundant teeth. It is also the only species of the mooneye family (Hiodontidae) occurring in Montana. The goldeye was first formally described and named in 1819, but Lewis probably should be given credit for its discovery.

### Sauger *Stizostedion canadensis*

Fish caught on the Missouri River above the mouth of the Marias River were identified by Elliott Coues as saugers, a species then already known to science.

Fig. 38. Channel catfish (top), blue catfish (middle), and cutthroat trout (bottom)

More recently, Ken Walcheck has suggested on the basis of their described tooth structure that this species might instead have been the flathead chub (*Hybopsis gracilis*), a much smaller species of fish.

Suckers *Catastomus* and *Prosopium* spp. FIG. 39

The suckers that were caught in the Missouri River of Montana by the expedition were identified by Elliott Coues as probably being the common northern (or longnose) sucker (*Catastomus catostomus*), a species then already known to science. One caught on the Yellowstone River on July 16, 1806, was identified by Coues as representing the then-undescribed mountain sucker (*Prosopium williamsoni*). The mountain sucker was not described until 1892, with specimens from western Montana. Both of these suckers are known to occur in the Yellowstone River.

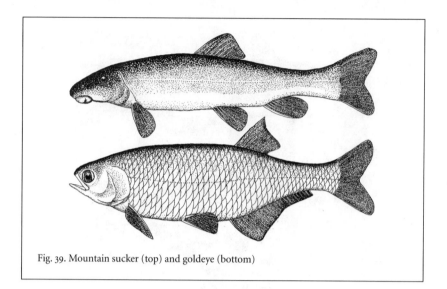

Fig. 39. Mountain sucker (top) and goldeye (bottom)

## Plants

### Black Greasewood  *Sarcobatus vermiculatus*

This shrub was the "pulpy leaf thorn" described by Lewis and Clark. Theirs is a good description, inasmuch as its leaves are fleshy and its rigid branches somewhat spiny. It is a widespread perennial shrub in alkaline soils, with leaves that are highly toxic to many animals but may be eaten during winter as an emergency food by some wild ungulates. Captain Lewis believed, incorrectly, that the greater sage-grouse also regularly consumed this plant's leaves. Native Americans sharpened the strong branches of this shrub and used them as digging tools. Collected July 20, 1806, in present-day Toole County, Montana.

### Blue Flax  *Linum lewisii*

This perennial plant, named in honor of Captain Lewis by Frederick Pursh, was collected July 9, 1806, perhaps in Beaverhead County, Montana. Lewis recognized that the stem of this plant produces strong fibers that might make "excellent flax." It was evidently used as such by Native Americans. A newly discovered species.

### Eastern Cottonwood  *Populus deltoides*

The herbarium specimen was presumably obtained in North or South Dakota if the indefinite date (August 1806) is correct. Cottonwood leaves and bark contain salicilin and populin, both precursors to the medicinally important aspirin. Not surprisingly, teas made from the bark of cottonwood were used by Native Americans for various ailments. Cottonwood trees were also extremely important to the success of the entire expedition, inasmuch as their fairly soft wood and the large size of the mature trees occurring along river edges made them excellent candidates for manufacturing dugout canoes. Ten of the 15 dugout canoes the expedition members constructed were made from cottonwoods, the others from ponderosa pine (*Pinus ponderosa*).

### Gumbo Evening Primrose   *Oenothera caespitosa*

This is a widespread perennial forb that is typical of badland soils and other nearly barren grounds. The roots of this and related species were used as external poultices for bruises, and the boiled root was used for a wide variety of ailments. The oils present in the seeds (such as linolenic acid) are also known to have physiological effects. Collected July 17, 1806, in present-day Cascade County, Montana. A newly discovered species.

### Needle-and-thread (Porcupine) Grass   *Stipa comata*

This species and wild rice are the only grasses represented in the Great Plains collections of Lewis and Clark, and surprisingly few other grasses were collected farther west. It is a common perennial species of mixed-grass prairies. Collected July 8, 1806, in Lewis and Clark County or Beaverhead County, Montana.

### Red False (Scarlet Globe) Mallow   *Sphaeralcea coccinea*

This is a widespread perennial forb. The Blackfoot used a paste made from chewing the plant stems and leaves as an external medicine for burns and sores. The Lakotas similarly made a paste to rub over their hands and arms, thus seemingly making them immune to the effects of scalding water. The "contrary medicine men" of the Lakotas used this purported protective trait to impress onlookers and encourage faith in their apparent special powers. Collected July 20, 1806, probably in present-day Toole County, Montana. A newly discovered species.

### Snow-on-the-Mountain   *Euphorbia marginata*

This is a widespread perennial forb on dry grasslands. Its leaves are somewhat poisonous, but they were used by the Dakotas as a basis for medicinal tea, which was used to treat mothers producing insufficient milk, and its crushed leaves were also used in warm water to make a kind of liniment. However, exposure of the skin to the milky sap can also cause severe inflammation. Collected July 28, 1806, along the Yellowstone River and in what is now Rosebud County, Montana. A newly discovered species.

5

# Lewis and Clark Sites of Biological and Historic Interest in the Central and Upper Missouri Valley

I n some cases the Lewis and Clark campsite locations mentioned below are uncertain and thus may be only approximate. The book by Ferris (1975) provides excellent descriptions of many of the more important historic sites mentioned here. For general information on national parks and recreation areas, use the National Park Service website, *www.nps.gov*. The home page of the Park Service's Lewis and Clark National Historic Trail is *www.nps.gov/lecl*. For useful travel information on national, state, and local historic and recreational sites, try *gorp.com* or *www.lewisandclarktrail.cjb.net*. The website of the Lewis and Clark Trail Heritage Foundation is *www.lewisandclark.org*. Local faunal checklists can often be obtained directly from the specific site's headquarters, but many such checklists may also be found on-line at the following Northern Prairie Wildlife Research Center website, *http://www.npwrc.usgs.gov/resource/ othrdata/chekbird/chekbird.htm*. A more general source of biological resource information on these and other sites is available at a related Northern Prairie website, *http://www.npwrc.usgs.gov/resource/type_C.htm*.

## Kansas and Northwestern Missouri

### Weston Bend State Park, Weston, Missouri
Located one mile south of Weston on State Highway 45, near the Lewis and Clark campsite of July 2, 1804. Riverbottom forest of mature hardwoods on the east side of the Missouri River. Camping is permitted.

### Weston Bend Bottomlands, Fort Leavenworth, Kansas
These bottomlands on the west side of the Missouri River across from Weston Bend State Park are on the 5,600-acre Fort Leavenworth military reserva-

tion. They consist of similar mature riverine stands of elm, hackberry, cotton-wood walnut, and pecan. Some of the trees are old enough to have been alive when Lewis and Clark camped near here on July 2, 1804. Accessible via Chief Joseph Loop Drive within Fort Leavenworth, Kansas. There are several hiking trails (such as Taildike Trail) leading through dense woods to the Missouri River. There is also a Frontier Army Museum at the fort and a Historical Society Museum.

## Lewis and Clark State Park, Rushville, Missouri

Located five miles south of Rushville, off State Highway 45, near the Lewis and Clark campsite of July 4, 1804. Mature riverine woodlands. The site contains an oxbow lake (Sugar Lake), a former channel in the Missouri that was cut off. It was first described by Lewis and Clark, who called it "Gosling Lake." Camping is permitted.

## Atchison, Kansas

Independence Park, on the city waterfront, marks the place where the expedition spent July 4, 1804, celebrating the national holiday and naming the small nearby creek Independence Creek.

## McCormack Loess Mounds Natural Area, Missouri

The 112-acre McCormack Loess Mounds is about 1.5 miles to the south of Squaw Creek National Wildlife Refuge (see below) and is near the Lewis and Clark campsite of July 10, 1804. This site is near the southern end of the Loess Hills region that extends along all of extreme western Iowa. The site is also the western half of the 227-acre J. C. McCormack Wildlife Area, and both overlook the Squaw Creek lowlands. Both sites are mostly upland prairie developed over loess-covered hills that rise as high as about 250 feet above the surrounding lowlands.

## Squaw Creek National Wildlife Refuge, Mound City, Missouri

Located five miles south of Mound City on U.S. Highway 159, near the Lewis and Clark campsite of July 11–12, 1804. A major waterfowl staging area in spring and fall, especially for snow geese, and visited later in the fall and during early spring by bald eagles. Also used by many other migratory water birds. Loess bluffs on the west side support prairie and mature hardwood forest. The refuge's bird checklist contains about 270 species, including such birds seen by Lewis and Clark in this general region as the American white pelican, common egret, American bittern, Canada goose, and wood duck. The refuge area comprises

6,887 acres, mostly consisting of riverbottom and upland forest, prairie, and marshes.

## Highland, Kansas

This small town in northeastern Kansas houses the Native American Heritage Museum and the Sac and Fox Tribal Museum. They contain exhibits documenting the impact of the Lewis and Clark expedition on the Native Americans living along the Missouri River, including the Iowa and Sac and Fox tribes. The relatively small, adjoining Iowa Indian Reservation and Sac and Fox Indian Reservation are located along the Nebraska-Kansas border, south of the Big Nemaha River. On the Nebraska side, about four miles south of Rulo, is a community hall of the Iowa tribe, housing some artifacts and historic as well as more recent Native American images. Not far north, along the Big Nemaha River and about 1.5 miles upstream from its mouth, is an ancient Iowa-Missouria burial ground. It was discovered on July 12, 1804, by Captain Clark, who described them as "Artificial Mounds." Traces of these ancient burial mounds still exist, but they have been largely obscured by more recent interments and agricultural activities. Clark also described the prairie grasses of the nearby bottomlands as about 4.5 feet tall, with clumps of "Osage Plumb," grapes, and wild cherries on the hillsides. Clark observed that the Big Nemaha ("Ne-Ma-Haw") was a meandering stream of clear water about 80 yards wide at its mouth. It is now a narrow, muddy stream with eroded silt banks.

## Brickyard Hill Loess Mound Natural Area, Missouri

This prairie preserve is reached by turning west off Exit 116 from I-29. It consists of 125 acres of Missouri's much larger 2,262-acre Brickyard Hill Conservation Area, which has extensive oak forests and 41 acres of intervening upland prairies along the loess bluffs, the so-called Bald-pated Hills of Lewis and Clark. Located near the Lewis and Clark campsite of July 13, 1804.

## Star School Hill Prairie Natural Area, Missouri

This native prairie site is located about 1.5 miles south of the Iowa state line and 12 miles north of Rockport. It is also about five miles northeast of the Brickyard Hill prairie preserve (see above). It lies on 70 acres of the adjoining Star School Hill Prairie Conservation Area, totaling 359 acres. Both are upland prairies situated on loess hills adjacent to the Missouri floodplain. Located near the Lewis and Clark campsite of July 13, 1804. On July 17 Captain Clark mentioned these "Bald Hills" and "extensive Prairie" that he observed in the vicinity of the present-day Missouri–Iowa state boundary.

## Nebraska and Iowa

### Rulo Bluffs Preserve, Nebraska

An undeveloped 424-acre forest, about six miles southeast of Rulo, containing mature hardwood forests and some prairie vegetation on high, steep loess hills and bluffs overlooking the Missouri River. It is noted for its high botanical diversity, but because the area is undeveloped, with no amenities or marked trails, access is restricted. Located near the Lewis and Clark campsite of July 11–12, 1804. Owned and managed by the Nature Conservancy; permission to enter must be obtained from their Omaha field office.

### Indian Cave State Park, Nebraska

A mostly wooded park of 2,831 acres, about ten miles east of Shubert, on State Highway 64E. Mature riverine hardwood forest. A shallow Paleozoic limestone cave of Pennsylvanian age contains a few Native American petroglyphs (mostly now overwhelmed by recent graffiti). There are 20 miles of hiking trails. Located near the Lewis and Clark campsite of July 14, 1804. Camping is permitted.

### Brownville, Nebraska

The expedition camped just south of here on July 15, 1804. The *Meriwether Lewis*, a now-retired steam-operated paddle-wheel dredge, is dry-docked in the city park beside the river, and has some Lewis and Clark information.

### Waubonsie State Park, Iowa

A 1,247-acre prairie and hardwood forest park, located on steep loess hills overlooking the Missouri River. At least one of the bur oaks in the park is known to be over 300 years old, so it was already mature when Lewis and Clark passed by these "bald-pated hills." At least ten acres are still in prairie vegetation. The park is nine miles north of Hamburg, off I-29 on State Highway 2. Camping is permitted. Located near the Lewis and Clark campsites of July 16–17, 1804.

### Nebraska City, Nebraska

A new facility, the Missouri River Basin Lewis and Clark Interpretive Trail and Visitor's Center, is currently being built. It is situated on 79 wooded acres, encompassing a tall, loess-capped bluff overlooking the Missouri River. It should be opened in time for the Lewis and Clark bicentennial and will emphasize the natural history of the expedition. Full-sized replicas of the Lewis and Clark keelboat and a pirogue (both authentically made for an IMAX documentary movie) will also be on display. Located near the Lewis and Clark campsite of July 17, 1804.

## Forney's Lake Wildlife Area, Iowa

This wildlife area is a state-owned wetland of 1,800 acres (400 acres of which is a refuge and the rest is open to sport hunting). Formerly an old Missouri River oxbow lake at the base of the Iowa Loess Hills, it is now a shallow cattail and tule marsh with wonderful spring habitat for migratory waterfowl (especially snow geese) and other wetland birds. It is reached by taking the Bartlett Exit from I-29, about 15 miles north of Waubonsie State Park (see above). Located near the Lewis and Clark campsite of July 18, 1804.

## Fontenelle Forest, Bellevue, Nebraska

A mature riverine hardwood forest of 1,400 acres, owned by the nonprofit Fontenelle Forest Association. It has 17 miles of hiking trails through upland and lowland woods, a visitor center, and a wetland learning center. There is a bird checklist of 246 species and a local mammal list. Located near the Lewis and Clark campsite of July 27, 1804.

## Neale Woods Nature Center, Omaha, Nebraska

A 554-acre nature preserve in northern Omaha, with mature upland oak-hickory forest, tallgrass prairie, nine miles of nature trails, and an interpretive center. An additional 262 acres of floodplain forest are being acquired. There is a bird checklist of about 190 species. Located near the Lewis and Clark campsite of July 28, 1804.

## Omaha, Nebraska

The Joslyn Art Museum has the entire collection of the magnificent watercolors made by Karl Bodmer during his trip up the Missouri River during the early 1830s with Alexander Philip Maximilian, Prince of Wied, just three decades after the Lewis and Clark expedition. Many of these originals were later converted into hand-colored aquatint engravings and published in Europe. An office of the Lewis and Clark National Historic Trail is located at 1709 Jackson Street, Omaha, Nebraska 68102.

## Lewis and Clark Monument, Council Bluffs, Iowa

A 40-acre site on the north side of Council Bluffs, commemorating the formal meeting of Lewis and Clark with the Otoe-Missourias. Natural habitats include oak-dominated woods and hillside prairies. On July 28, 1804, Captain Clark reported seeing "high prairie and hills, with timber" near present-day Council Bluffs. Folsom Point Preserve, a 281-acre Nature Conservancy prairie in the Loess Hills, is located at the south side of Council Bluffs off Brohard Avenue. Council Bluffs is also home to the Western Historic Trails Center, providing information on the Lewis and Clark Historic Trail and other western trails such as the Oregon and Mormon Trails. About eight miles north of Council Bluffs, off State Highway 183, is Hitchcock Nature Center, a Pottawattamie County educational facility. It is located on the crest of a series of 400-foot loess hills and is noted as a site for watching fall raptor migrations along the Missouri Valley. The "Councile Bluff" site that was selected by Lewis and Clark for their historic meeting with the Otoe-Missourias is located about 15 miles north of the city of Council Bluffs, Iowa, and is on the Nebraska side of the river (see Fort Atkinson below).

## Boyer Chute National Wildlife Refuge, Fort Calhoun, Nebraska

A new and rather small (2,000-acre) refuge located about five miles east of Fort Calhoun, near the Lewis and Clark campsite of July 28, 1804. This is a reconstructed side channel (a so-called chute) on the west side of the Missouri River. The area is still under development, with an additional 8,000 acres planned. There is no local bird checklist, but the DeSoto Bend refuge list is probably applicable. Managed by the nearby DeSoto Bend National Wildlife Refuge (see below).

## Fort Atkinson State Historical Park, Fort Calhoun, Nebraska

Located one mile north of Fort Calhoun on County Road 34, near the Lewis and Clark campsite of July 30–August 3, 1804. Fort Atkinson was founded in 1820 but was soon abandoned in 1827, when western overland routes farther south made the Missouri River corridor less vital to national interests. Fort restoration began in the 1960s, and there are now several restored buildings as well as a visitor center. The fort is located on the summit of Council Bluff (on the Nebraska side of the river, not in Iowa), the place where Lewis and Clark met with the Otoe-Missourias on August 3, 1804. (As a result of channel shifting, the river is now some three miles east of the bluff summit, and because of timber growth is no longer visible from the bluff.) This was Lewis and Clark's first formal meeting with any tribe of Native Americans. The Otoe-Missourias were initially assigned a reservation area of 160,000 acres along the present-day Nebraska-Kansas border but in 1881 were relocated to Indian Territory (now parts of Noble and Pawnee Counties in Oklahoma). It was the Otoe (often spelled Oto) who were responsible for giving Nebraska its name, from an Otoe word meaning "flat water," referring to the Platte River.

## DeSoto Bend National Wildlife Refuge, Missouri Valley, Iowa

A 7,823-acre federal refuge situated one mile east of Blair, Nebraska, on an old oxbow of the Missouri River. This refuge is a major spring and fall staging area for snow geese and other migratory waterfowl. A visitor center contains panoramic viewing windows and a vast collection of artifacts from the unlucky steamboat *Bertrand*, sunk when it hit a snag in 1865. It had been filled with household goods and mining supplies intended for the Montana gold fields. The refuge has a bird checklist of 240 species, including such species seen by Lewis and Clark in this general region as the great blue heron, bald eagle, wild turkey, and western meadowlark. Located near the Lewis and Clark campsite of August 3, 1804.

## Lewis and Clark State Park, Onawa, Iowa

A small (176-acre) state park situated five miles west of Onawa on State Highway 15. The oxbow lake is surrounded by cottonwoods and other river-ine hardwoods, with a reconstructed full-sized keelboat and two pirogues on view during the summer months. Encompasses the Lewis and Clark campsite of August 9, 1804. A new interpretive center should be finished in 2003. Just east of Onawa is Sylvan Runkel State Preserve, a 330-acre tallgrass prairie within the 2,742-acre Loess Hills Wildlife Management Area. Monona County has two other public-access natural areas, Loess Hills State Forest, with more than 100 acres of prairie, and Turin Loess Hills, with 220 acres.

## Pelican Point State Recreation Area, Nebraska

Pelican Point State Recreation Area is close to the place where a vast flock of American white pelicans was seen by the expedition. "Pelican Island" is no longer an island, but the point is located four miles east and four miles north of Tekamah.

## Omaha and Winnebago Indian Reservations

These two reservations, located between Decatur and Homer, Nebraska, were established in 1856 and 1866, respectively, the Winnebagos having been moved here from South Dakota and, still earlier, from Minnesota. Standing on the Omaha Indian Reservation is Blackbird Hill, the gravesite of the Omaha chief Blackbird, which was visited by Lewis and Clark on August 11, 1804. Chief Blackbird had died of smallpox in 1800 and was buried sitting erect on a horse, and a wooden pole decorated with all of the scalps he had taken was planted in the soil above. His gravesite is situated on the highest of the river bluffs between Decatur and Macy but is not readily accessible. The 300-foot and now mostly tree-covered promontory can best be seen about one mile east of Blackbird Scenic Overview at a site three miles north of Decatur (milepost 152 on U.S. Highway 75).

The Omahas had moved into the region from the Ohio River valley by the

1700s, and by 1775 the tribe had a large village in this immediate area. During the smallpox epidemic of 1800 the Omaha population was reduced from about 700 to 300, and its previous reputation as a powerful warrior society disappeared. During the later period of displacement of Native Americans to reservations in the mid-1800s, the Omahas were allowed to remain on part (originally 300,000 acres) of their original homeland. The northern part of their ceded land was later given to the Winnebagos, and some of the remainder was later sold to white settlers. In spite of their peaceful nature the Omahas were not accepted as U.S. citizens until 1887, and their full rights of citizenship were not attained until 1924. Similarly, the Pawnees of eastern Nebraska (the "Pani" or "Pania" of Lewis and Clark) were sent in the 1850s to a relatively tiny preserve of about 300 square miles along the Loup River (now part of Nance County), an area representing less than 1 percent of their original vast homeland along the Platte Valley. After this land was sold to settlers in 1872 they were relocated in 1874 to a part of Indian Territory (Oklahoma), in an area between the Arkansas and Cimarron Rivers. At the time of Lewis and Clark, the Pawnees were probably second only to the Lakotas in population size among Plains natives, numbering perhaps 10,000 people. By comparison, the Omahas may have historically numbered about 2,800 at maximum, the Otoes about 1,800, and the Missourias about 500. By the late 1900s there were still nearly 3,000 Natives Americans living on Nebraska reservations, including about 1,300 Omahas, 1,100 Winnebagos, and about 400 Santees. The annual powwow of the Winnebago tribe occurs in late July.

## Sioux City, Iowa

This city, built near the Lewis and Clark campsite of August 20, 1804, has a Lewis and Clark Interpretive Center in Chris Larsen Park as well as the Sergeant Floyd Monument, which is placed on a hilltop south of town near where Sgt. Charles Floyd, the only expedition fatality, was buried. Because of erosion, his remains were reburied twice, once in 1857 and again in 1900, this time in the concrete foundation of the monument. Floyd River runs nearby, and the Sergeant Floyd Riverboat Welcome Center, a dry-docked diesel inspection ship, has been converted into a small museum of Missouri River history, including information on Lewis and Clark. At the northern edge of Sioux City on Memorial Drive is Stone State Park, a 1,069-acre prairie and woodland reserve situated on loess hills overlooking the confluence of the Big Sioux and Missouri Rivers. It has a nature trail, a demonstration prairie, and an available list of local wildflowers. Dorothy Pecaut Nature Center, with exhibits on the Loess Hills region, is within the park. Nearby is Sioux City Prairie, a 150-acre tallgrass prairie west of Briar Cliff College, and Mount Talbot State Preserve, off Talbot Road. About ten miles north of Sioux City is the 889-acre Five-Ridge Prairie, and near there is the 2,000-acre Broken Kettle Prairie, the largest of the tallgrass prairie preserves in Iowa. Both are Nature Conservancy preserves.

The loess hills in northern Iowa (Woodbury and Monona Counties) may approach 400 feet in height and range up to ten miles wide, the loess caps themselves adding as much as about 200 feet to the underlying sedimentary substrate. The Loess Hills region of Iowa comprises the eastern edge of the Missouri Valley, and it supports over 100 nesting species of birds, 54 mammals, 24 reptiles, and 10 amphibians, according to a summary by Cornelia Mutel. There are also at least 39 native species of trees and larger shrubs in the Loess Hills, the botanical diversity gradually increasing from north to south. These hills are the second-highest accumulations of windblown materials ("loess" is a German term for "loose") in the world. The silt-sized particles that were deposited here originated much farther west, and a layer of loess several feet thick covers all of Iowa except for the north-central section. The hills still support up to 20,000 acres of native tallgrass prairies, much of which exist in small, diminishing patches.

Near North Sioux City (take Exit 4 from I-29) and bordering the Missouri River is Adams Homestead and Nature Preserve, a 1,500-acre state-owned park and preserve with 7.5 miles of crushed limestone trails and 5.5 miles of grassy trails, mostly through lowland riverine woods.

## Ponca State Park, Ponca, Nebraska

A state park of 830 acres, situated two miles north of Ponca, on State Highway 12. Consists of mature riverine hardwood forest at the lower end of the Missouri National Recreational River system. There are 17 miles of hiking trails. A new interpretive center, the Missouri National Recreational River Resource and Educational Center, has been constructed in Ponca State Park and focuses on the ecology and history of the Missouri River, including the Lewis and Clark expedition. There is a park bird checklist of about 240 species. Located near the Lewis and Clark campsite of August 22, 1804. Camping is permitted. The park was named after the Ponca tribe, once part of the Omaha tribe, which had settled on the west bank of the Missouri River in present-day South Dakota during the early 1700s. At the time of Lewis and Clark, the Poncas numbered perhaps 800 people. Their initial reservation (first established in 1858 and enlarged to 96,000 acres in 1865) was taken over in 1868 by the federal government without prior consultation and was made part of the Great Sioux Reservation. The resulting conflicts with the Lakotas, together with a government eviction order in 1876, forced the Poncas to resettle in Indian Territory (now Oklahoma). They were first assigned to the then-existing Quapaw Agency during the winter of 1877–78. The return of Chief Standing Bear only a year later with about

30 of his followers to bury his eldest son in an ancestral graveyard led to the entire group's arrest. It produced one of the most famous courtroom scenes in American history and raised the remarkable legal question as to whether a Native American was a "person" under the meaning of then-existing law. The case against Standing Bear was eventually dismissed by the Supreme Court, and a restoration of 26,236 acres of Ponca tribal land in the Niobrara Valley occurred in 1881, after a presidential commission reviewed the tribe's sad history. In 1884 the Oklahoma (or "Hot Country") Poncas were moved to a new reservation in the Salt Fork River area. This group is now located in Kay and Noble Counties of Oklahoma. However, the Ponca reservation in Nebraska was dissolved in 1954, and for several decades the tribe was no longer recognized by the federal government, until it was officially restored again in 1990.

## Volcano Hill Historic Site

Newcastle, Nebraska, is five miles southwest of a bluff called the Ionia Volcano, which Captain Clark reported he had touched and found unaccountably warm. The heat was later judged to be produced by the oxidation of shale.

## Niobrara State Park, Niobrara, Nebraska

This 1,632-acre park is located one mile north of Niobrara on State Highway 12 and mostly consists of mature riverine hardwood forest, not greatly altered from the area's natural state. It is situated at the now-impounded mouth of the Niobrara River, 20 miles of which are now part of the Missouri National Recreational River system. There is a two-mile trail along the entire northern boundary of the park and an interpretive center with some Lewis and Clark exhibits. Located near the Lewis and Clark campsite of September 4, 1804. Camping is permitted.

East of Niobrara State Park is the Santee Sioux Indian Reservation, whose ancestors were brought there in 1869 from the Crow Creek Reservation in western South Dakota. Still earlier, they had been removed from Minnesota. There they had engaged in a bloody uprising against the white settlers in 1862, after which 1,800 Santees were imprisoned and 33 executed. The Santee Sioux reservation in Nebraska originally consisted of 117,000 acres but was later substantially reduced.

## The Cupola

This treeless sedimentary cone of grayish-yellow clays, about 70 feet in height, was discovered and named "The Cupola" by expedition members on September 7, 1804. Now known as "Old Baldy," this largely intact site is seven miles north of Lynch, Nebraska, on privately owned land. The nearest public road (unnumbered but easily traveled) passes within about a half mile and offers an excellent view of the site and several miles of the nearby river valley, which is still fairly pristine. At the base of this promontory a colony of black-tailed prairie dogs was discovered by Lewis and Clark, the first examples of this keystone shortgrass plains species known to science. This colony is now gone, but others occur in the general vicinity. Several prairie dogs that Lewis and Clark had captured alive were sent back to Washington DC in April of 1805, one of which survived the 4,000-mile trip. It and a black-billed magpie that had likewise survived were eventually displayed alive for a time at Charles W. Peale's Philadelphia Museum (also known as Peale's Museum), which eventually received nearly all the Lewis and Clark specimens at the end of the expedition. It was housed in Independence Hall until 1838, when it was moved the first of two times. Finally, in 1850 its contents were sold, in part to P. T. Barnum and in part to the Boston Museum. Some of the materials from the latter eventually were passed on to Harvard University, but most have disappeared, including the prairie dog.

## South Dakota

### Missouri National Recreational River

The lower section of this nationally designated part of the Missouri is located along the Lewis and Clark campsites of August 22–25, 1804. This 59-mile segment of river stretching from about Yankton to Ponca State Park still somewhat resembles the river conditions seen by Lewis and Clark. The Yankton Sioux Indian Reservation (now about 36,000 acres) is located directly north of the river. It has been home to the Nakota-dialect (Yankton) Sioux, who first formally met Lewis and Clark in the vicinity of present-day Yankton, South Dakota. The reservation-based population in the early 1990s was about 3,000 people, with another 3,000 living off the reservation. At the time of Lewis and Clark, the Sioux were the most numerous of the plains tribes, at one time numbering perhaps as many as 27,000.

### Spirit Mound

Seven miles north of Vermillion on the west side of State Highway 19 is Spirit Mound, a low, treeless promontory climbed by Captain Clark and a small party on August 25, 1804, and from which they saw large herds of elk and bison. Long neglected, this 320-acre site has been acquired by the South Dakota Game and Fish Department, which is restoring the site to native vegetation. In the city of Vermillion the W. H. Over Museum has a Lewis and Clark–Spirit Mound Learning and Information Center. Associated with it is a Heritage Garden featuring plants observed or collected by Lewis and Clark. The Vermillion River's name comes from the red clay pigments along its banks. The nearby 39-mile section of the Missouri from Fort Randall Dam south to the confluence of the Niobrara River is also a part of the Missouri National Recreational River (see above) and encompasses the Lewis and Clark campsites of September 4–8, 1804. About 30 miles north of Vermillion is Sioux Falls, which has the Center for Western Studies at Augustana College as well as the Washington Pavilion of Arts and Sciences housing both Native American and regional art galleries.

## Lewis and Clark State Recreation Area

This 1,227-acre state recreation area, adjoining the 32,000-acre Lewis and Clark Reservoir and Gavins Point Dam, encompasses the Lewis and Clark campsites of August 28 to September 1, 1804. Calumet Bluff, where Lewis and Clark met formally with the Yankton Sioux, is located on the Nebraska side of the river, about two miles east of Gavins Point Dam. This bluff, about 170 to 180 feet high, is part of a series of steep-sided reddish- to brownish-clay promontories on both sides of the river. Calumet Bluff is now the site of a Lewis and Clark Visitor Center, which contains exhibits on the river, the Lewis and Clark expedition, and the council held with the Yankton Sioux. A nearby nature trail is 1.5 miles long. At the western end of the reservoir on the Nebraska side is a lowland area of woods and wetlands, the Bazille Creek Wildlife Management Area, totaling 4,500 acres. Camping is permitted at the state recreation area. Yankton has an annual Lewis and Clark Festival on Labor Day weekend.

## Randall Creek Recreation Area and Karl Mundt National Wildlife Refuge, Pickstown

Karl Mundt NWR is a small federal refuge located immediately below Fort Randall Dam and Lake Francis Case. It was established to protect wintering bald eagles, so public access may be restricted. However, an eagle-watching platform is located at Randall Creek Recreation Area, about three miles north of the refuge and near the south end of Fort Randall Dam. Karl Mundt NWR is located near the now-impounded Lewis and Clark campsite of September 8, 1804, and is managed by Lakes Andes National Wildlife Refuge.

## Lake Andes National Wildlife Refuge

This refuge is located six miles east of the town of Lake Andes, beside an oxbow lake of the same name. It consists of 5,770 acres, in three separate units, mostly of marshes and prairie along the lake's shorelines. There is a bird checklist of 213 species. Bird species occurring here and that were observed by Lewis and Clark while they were in the Great Plains include the American white pelican, bald eagle, greater prairie-chicken, sharp-tailed grouse, great horned owl, and cliff swallow.

## Snake Creek State Recreation Area

A 735-acre area located on impounded Lake Francis Case. It is directly west of Platte via State Highway 44. Near the now-flooded Lewis and Clark campsite of September 11, 1804. Camping is permitted. The Platte Creek State Recreation area is located about eight miles farther south, near the Lewis and Clark campsite of September 10, 1804. Camping is permitted.

## Chamberlain

The Lewis and Clark Keelboat Information Center is a newly finished, state-operated tourist information center located just off I-90 near the bridge crossing Lake Francis Case. The Center is devoted largely to Lewis and Clark, with a somewhat simplified keelboat reconstruction that has been incorporated into the structure of the building itself. Exhibits feature some of the supplies carried on the expedition, its regional discoveries, and excellent murals showing historical aspects of the expedition. The Information Center also has surrounding native vegetation and provides a spectacular overview of Lake Francis Case. Chamberlain's other historic and cultural attractions include the Atka Lakota Museum and Cultural Center, a modern Native American museum and art gallery with both historic and recent Lakota cultural items. Chamberlain is located near the Lewis and Clark campsite of September 18, 1804. Two miles north of town on South Dakota Highway 50 is Roam Free Park, with two nature trails and native grassland vegetation.

## Lower Brule and Crow Creek Indian Reservations

These large reservations (Lower Brule Indian Reservation is 132,601 acres; Crow Creek Indian Reservation is 125,591 acres) border both sides of the impounded Missouri River (Lake Sharpe) in the region of the Big Bend for about 80 miles of shoreline distance. These reservations are home to the Lower Brule and Crow Creek components of the Lakotas. A Native American National Scenic Byway (Bureau of Indian Affairs Highways 10 and 4) crosses both reservations, linking Chamberlain and Pierre. This near-wilderness road passes scenic rolling hills that are often capped with infertile blackish Pierre shales of Cretaceous age. The soils support arid-adapted plants such as some of the sages that were discovered by Lewis and Clark. The two reservations collectively encompass the Lewis and Clark outward-bound campsites of September 19–22, 1804, and the return campsites of August 26 and 27, 1806. There are summer powwows (in August), and the reservation lands support large tribal bison herds. Fort Kiowa, built in 1822, was located just south of the Lower Brule Reservation, and Fort Defiance, built in 1842, was located within it, as was Fort Hale. These forts as well as Fort Thompson and Fort Pierre were once important jumping-off points for prospectors headed for the Black Hills.

## West Bend State Recreation Area

A 154-acre state-owned recreational site along the famous Big Bend of the Missouri, now a part of impounded Lake Sharpe, formed behind Big Bend Dam. The historic river length of the Big Bend was 30 miles, but the overland distance between the two ends of the loop was only about 2,000 yards. The state recreation area is located 35 miles southeast of Pierre, off State Highway 34, and is near the Lewis and Clark campsite of September 20, 1804. Camping is permitted.

## Fort Pierre National Grassland

Headquartered at Pierre. A large (115,996-acre) federally owned area of short-grass and mixed-grass prairie, with an associated bird checklist of more than 200 species. Many gravel roads intersect the grassland, where western mead-owlarks, upland sandpipers, and marbled godwits are among the more characteristic breeding birds. Lark buntings, possibly but not definitely seen by Lewis and Clark, are usually very common. There is no published mammal list, but the white-tailed jackrabbit, thirteen-lined ground squirrel, black-tailed prairie dog, bushy-tailed woodrat, coyote, mule deer, and pronghorn all occur in this general area, to mention some of the regional mammals discovered by Lewis and Clark. Camping is permitted. The northern boundary is located about ten miles south of Fort Pierre and may be reached via U.S. Highway 83.

## Farm Island State Recreation Area, Pierre

A state-owned 1,235-acre nature preserve and recreational area, located near the Lewis and Clark campsite of September 24, 1804. A hiking trail extends from Pierre south to the recreation area along the east shoreline of the Missouri River. Camping is permitted.

## LaFramboise Island National Recreation Trail, Pierre

A 1,280-acre recreational area and nature preserve (including an eight-mile nature trail loop). Its entrance is located near Steamboat Park, off Poplar Avenue, and near the Lewis and Clark campsite of September 25, 1804. It was at the nearby mouth of the Bad ("Teton") River, along the west shore of the Missouri River (now a Fort Pierre city park), that the Corps of Discovery met three Lakota (Brule) chiefs and their warriors. It proved to be a danger-fraught encounter that led to threats and near-bloodshed over gifts and trading procedures, probably caused or at least exacerbated by translation problems. Also in Pierre is the South Dakota Cultural Heritage Center, with such items as an Arikara bullboat, a tipi, a stunning war-pony effigy, and examples of Native American beadwork. There is also a replica of the Jefferson peace medals carried by Lewis and Clark.

## Fort Sully Game Refuge, Lake Oahe

A state-owned wildlife preserve, located on a peninsula on the east shore of Lake Oahe, about 30 miles west of Onida, via 185th Street, and near the Lewis and Clark outward-bound campsite of October 1, 1804, as well as the return campsite of August 24, 1806. North of Onida and west of Gettysburg, off State Highway 1804 and U.S. Highway 212, is West Whitlock State Recreation Area, where a full-sized replica of an Arikara earth lodge has been constructed.

## Mobridge

Located near the Lewis and Clark campsites of October 8–10, 1804. It was here that the first Arikara ("Rikara") village was encountered by Lewis and Clark, at the mouth of the Grand River. A smallpox epidemic in 1780–81 had already killed most of the population of perhaps originally as many as 30,000 people. By 1800 the Arikaras consisted of about 3,800 persons. Like the Pawnees, they were part of the Caddoan-language group. The quite different Siouan language group comprised a large, multitribal assemblage, including the Lakota and Dakota, Mandan, Hidatsa, Ponca, Omaha, Missouria, and Kansa tribes. A monument to Sacagawea is located on the west side of Lake Oahe near Mobridge. It is on the Standing Rock Indian Reservation (see below), about six miles west of Mobridge on U.S. Highway 12 and four miles south on South Dakota Highway 1806. Sacagawea evidently spent the last part of her relatively short life of about 25 years in the vicinity of Fort Manuel, a Missouri Fur Company post that was located in what is now Corson County, South Dakota, near the present North Dakota border. She died in December 1812, not long after giving birth to a daughter, Lizette. Although her exact burial site is unknown, it has probably been covered by Lake Oahe. After the death of his mother, Jean Baptiste spent a few years with Captain Clark in St. Louis but later traveled abroad, became a mountain man and guide, and died of pneumonia at the age of 61 in Oregon. About a hundred yards away is a huge (seven-ton) granite bust of Sitting Bull, the great Lakota chief of the Indian wars, who was reburied here in 1953 after an initial interment at Fort Yates, North Dakota. He had surrendered in 1881 and been brought to Fort Union, North Dakota, several years after fleeing to Canada with the survivors of his Hunkpapa community. Sitting Bull spent most of the period from 1883 to 1890 at the Standing Rock reservation. In 1890 he was shot and killed there, together with his son and six policemen, while he was being detained by American Indian police, having been falsely accused of fostering the messianic Ghost Dance ritual then sweeping the western plains. This episode happened a year after Dakota Territory was divided into the present states of North and South Dakota.

## Pocasse National Wildlife Refuge, Columbia

A federal refuge of 2,585 acres and a subimpoundment of Lake Oahe. It is a major migration staging area for waterfowl and sandhill cranes, but there is not yet a bird checklist available. Located near the Lewis and Clark campsite of October 12, 1804.

## Cheyenne River and Standing Rock Indian Reservations

The enormous Cheyenne River Indian Reservation (1.4 million acres) borders the west side of Lake Oahe for much of its length, and is home to four bands of Lakotas. This reservation encompasses the Lewis and Clark campsites of October 10–12, 1804. The even larger Standing Rock Indian Reservation (2,328,534 acres), current home to some of the Dakota- and Lakota-dialect branches of the Sioux nation, continues along the west shoreline into southwestern North Dakota, north to about 25 miles beyond Fort Yates. The reservation was named for a rock that is sacred to the Arikaras and Lakotas and whose form resembles that of a seated woman. It is located across from the Agency Headquarters at Fort Yates. The reservation encompasses the Lewis and Clark outward-bound campsites of October 14–17, 1804, and the return campsites of August 20–21, 1806. There are annual summer powwows (held in July at Standing Rock, in August at Cheyenne River) and tribal bison herds. Before the Civil War all of South Dakota west of the Missouri was made part of a vast Sioux Indian reservation, but in the 1870s the federal government violated its own treaty and subdivided it. Much of this region was then taken from the Sioux, including their sacred Black Hills, where gold had been discovered during General Custer's military survey in 1874. There are still nearly 5 million acres of reservation lands in South Dakota, totaling nine reservations and supporting about 57,000 residents, counting three reservations whose boundaries extend into Nebraska or North Dakota. The Pine Ridge and Rosebud Reservations of southwestern South Dakota support the state's largest number of reservation members, the Oglala and Brule, both composing part of the Lakotas. Other groups live on the Cheyenne River, Standing Rock, and the Wood Mountain (in Canada) Reservations. The western Lakota group comprised seven major subgroups or tribal bands, including such famous names as the Oglala, Brule, and Hunkpapa. Under the leadership of chiefs like Crazy Horse and Sitting Bull, the men of these bands took their long-awaited revenge on General Custer at the Battle of Little Bighorn. The middle group included the Yankton and the Yanktonai subgroups. The major tribal subgroups of the eastern Dakotas included the Sisseton, Wahpeton, Wahpekute, and Mdewakantonwon.

## North Dakota

### Huff Indian Village State Historic Site

An unrestored ancient Mandan village, located one mile south of Huff, near the Lewis and Clark campsite of October 19, 1804, and just off State Highway 1806. (Conveniently for aiding Lewis and Clark fans' memories, North Dakota Highway 1804 traces the expedition's 1804 outward-bound route along the east and north side of the Missouri River. Highway 1806 similarly follows the expedition's return route in 1806, along the south and west side of the river. This same highway numbering arrangement also applies to South Dakota.)

### Fort Abraham Lincoln State Park

This state park is seven miles south of Mandan on State Highway 1806. Nearby is the partially restored On-A-Slant Indian Village, an ancient Mandan site occupied at the mouth of the Heart River for two centuries, or until about 1740, and supporting a maximum population about 1,500 Mandans. By 1764 the villagers had moved north to join the Hidatsas near the Knife River. At the time of Lewis and Clark, the entire Mandan tribe numbered perhaps 3,600 people, as compared with about 2,500 Hidatsas (or Minitari; the "Minnetaree" of Lewis and Clark). Compared with the Mandans, the Hidatsas were relatively fierce, often fighting at the extreme western end of their range with the Shoshones. In one of these encounters they captured Sacagawea, then still only about ten years old. Smallpox struck the Upper Missouri tribes in 1837, when it was brought upstream by an American Fur Company supply ship, further reducing the Mandan population to only about 150. Four full-sized Mandan earth lodges have been reconstructed, and there is evidence of 75 ancient lodge sites. There is also a visitor center with Mandan cultural objects and replicas of some Lewis and Clark items. During the Indian wars of the 1870s, Gen. George Armstrong Custer and the Seventh Calvary were stationed here prior to their ill-fated military campaign of 1876. The fort was built in 1872 and was abandoned in 1891 after the Indian wars, but many buildings have been reconstructed. Located eight miles south of Mandan, on State Highway 1806, it is near the Lewis and Clark outward-bound campsite of October 20, 1804, which was used again during the return phase of the expedition on August 18, 1806. From about this point north to the Garrison Dam there are nearly 100 miles of fairly free-flowing river. Camping is permitted at the state park.

## Double Ditch Indian Village State Historic Site

This unrestored Mandan village, seven miles north of Bismarck on State Highway 1804, dates back to about 1500, and was abandoned after a smallpox epidemic in the early 1780s. There is a self-guided walk. Located near the Lewis and Clark campsite of October 22, 1804.

## Cross Ranch Nature Preserve, Hensler

This 6,000-acre Nature Conservancy preserve is located about ten miles south of Washburn, off State Highway 200A, or six miles southeast of Hensler. It is largely comprised of mixed-grass prairie, with bison and other typical high plains wildlife. A bird checklist of 147 species is available for the preserve. Species occurring here that were observed by Lewis and Clark while they were in the Great Plains include the sharp-tailed grouse, wild turkey, red-headed wood-pecker, black-billed magpie, and western meadowlark. Over 100 species of wild-flowers are known to occur at the preserve, and there is a nine-mile hiking and nature trail. There is also a captive bison herd. Ancient sites of Mandan and Minitari villages are also present. Located near the Lewis and Clark outward-bound campsite of October 24, 1804, and the return campsite of August 17, 1806. The nearby Cross Ranch State Park encompasses 589 acres. Camping is permit-ted in the state park.

## Fort Clark State Historic Site, Stanton

Located about eight miles southeast of Stanton on State Highway Alt 200. Fort Clark was built in 1830 to help serve a Mandan village that had been estab-lished in 1822. The village was abandoned after a smallpox epidemic in 1837 but was reoccupied from 1838 to 1860 by the Arikaras. There are some remains of the fort visible, which burned in 1861, as well as those of an earth-lodge village, and a burial ground.

## Fort Mandan Historic Site and Lewis and Clark Interpretive Center, Washburn

Fort Mandan Historic Site is located 2.5 miles west of Washburn on North Dakota County Road 17, close to the junction of U.S. Highway 83 and State Highway 100A, and 1.5 miles west of the Lewis and Clark Interpretive Center. The Interpretive Center has a cottonwood dugout canoe of the type used by Lewis and Clark, as well as other items similar to those used by the expedition. The original Fort Mandan was built a few miles southeast of present-day Stanton, on the northeast side of the Missouri River, and close to three Hidatsa (two Minitari, one Amahami) and two Mandan villages. The fort was largely destroyed by a prairie fire before the expedition's return in 1806. When the expedition returned in mid-August of 1806, Sacagawea (the preferred North Dakota spelling is Sakakawea, based on the original Hidatsa), her son, and Charbonneau all remained behind, as did John Coulter. Coulter later became one of the West's most famous mountain men. Charbonneau remained with the Mandans and Hidatsas for most of his long life, serving in part as an interpreter and also acting as a guide to Prince Maximilian in the 1830s. There is a Fort Mandan Overlook State Historic Site 11.5 miles west of Washburn on State Highway 200A that provides a view of the actual fort's vicinity. A reconstruction of original Fort Mandan has been erected on a 30-acre site about ten miles downstream from the expedition's actual 1804–5 wintering site. The Lewis and Clark Interpretive Center in Washburn emphasizes the winter of 1804–5 that the Corps spent at Fort Mandan and features a complete set of Karl Bodmer prints depicting the Upper Missouri region and its inhabitants during the 1830s. The McLean County Historical Society Museum on Washburn's Main Street also has some Lewis and Clark displays. On the north side of Lake Sakakawea (three miles south of Garrison) is Fort Stevenson State Park, with some expedition exhibits. The eastern end of the lake (east of U.S. Highway 83) is Audubon National Wildlife Refuge (see below).

## Knife River Indian Villages National Historic Site, Stanton

Located on State Highway 31, one-half mile north of Stanton, and in the general vicinity of the expedition's wintering site at Fort Mandan in 1804–5 and their return campsites of August 13–16, 1806. A bird checklist of 212 species is available, and there is a nature trail. Species occurring here that were observed by Lewis and Clark while in the Great Plains include the Canada goose, sharp-tailed grouse, wild turkey, piping plover, black-billed magpie, and loggerhead shrike. The five villages at this site once held a maximum of 3,000 to 5,000 Mandans and Hidatsas, and it was at one of them (the upstream Hidatsa village) that Sacagawea was living with Charbonneau at the time of Lewis and Clark's visit. There is archeological evidence of some 9,000 years of occupation of the site. Near the visitor center is a reconstructed Hidatsa earth lodge, and there are also the remains of at least 60 ancient earth lodges, abandoned around 1780 following a smallpox epidemic. The largest site, the 15-acre Big Hidatsa Village (also known as the Upper Minitari village or Olds archeological site), is a National Historic Landmark. It contains the remains of more than 100 earth lodges and countless bone fragments from bison and other animals. A Northern Plains Indian Culture Fest is held here annually in late July. A United Tribes International Powwow is also held annually in Bismarck, usually during the weekend following Labor Day.

## Audubon National Wildlife Refuge, Coleharbor

This large federal refuge of 14,735 acres surrounds and includes a subimpoundment of Lake Sakakawea (10,421 acres). It lies about ten miles to the east of the Lewis and Clark campsites of April 7–8, 1805. There is a species checklist of 239 birds, 37 mammals, 5 reptiles, 3 amphibians, and 37 fish. Bird species occurring here that were observed by Lewis and Clark in the Great Plains include the American white pelican, American bittern, sharp-tailed grouse, American avocet, willet, horned lark, and western meadowlark. Mammals occurring in the area and that were evidently also seen by Lewis and Clark include the thirteen-lined and Richardson's ground squirrels, coyote, northern pocket gopher, and white-tailed jackrabbit. Pronghorns are sometimes common. Blinds are available for nature observation and photography, and there is an eight-mile interpretive trail. About 15 miles east of Audubon National Wildlife Refuge, to the east of Turtle Lake, is the John E. Williams Nature Preserve, with several alkali lakes and one of the largest populations of piping plovers in the country.

## Fort Berthold Indian Reservation

This very large reservation (about 1 million acres) occupies much of both sides of Lake Sakakawea, which has impounded 368,000 acres and has 1,600 miles of shoreline. It is home to the Arikaras, Hidatsas (Minitaris), and Mandans, all well known to Lewis and Clark. Fort Berthold was built in 1845 by the American Fur Company as a trading post, to be near the Mandan and Hidatsa villages then being established about 60 river miles upstream from Fort Mandan. The reservation encompasses the Lewis and Clark campsites of April 10–15, 1805. Near the north end of the reservation and 11 miles west of New Town on U.S. Highway 23 is Four Bears Park. A reservation museum (the Three Tribes Museum) near New Town is run by the Three Affiliated Tribes. It details the history of the Arikaras, Mandans, and Hidatsas, including their encounters with Lewis and Clark, and features a reconstructed full-sized earth lodge. Three miles south of New Town on North Dakota Highway 23 is Crow Flies High Butte Historic Site and associated exhibits. The top of this butte provides a panoramic view of the nearby badlands and upland topography; the river valley itself is now entirely impounded. The butte is named for a Hidatsa chief who founded a nearby village. It was approximately at this point that Captain Lewis and his party finally caught up with Captain Clark's group during the return phase of the expedition, on August 12, 1806. There are annual powwows at the Fort Berthold Reservation during June, July, and August.

## Little Missouri National Grassland and Theodore Roosevelt National Park

The northern section of the grassland is located near the Lewis and Clark campsite of April 15, 1805. It is only part of a vast region (1,027,852 acres) of federally owned shortgrass prairies and badlands that in part extend to the south shore of Lake Sakakawea. This relatively small section is located generally to the north of Keene and is best reached by taking State Highway 1806 east and north from Watford City. A larger section of this enormous national grassland, the largest federally owned grassland in the United States, lies along the Little Missouri River. It is headquartered in Dickinson. Theodore Roosevelt National Park (70,416 acres) is located in two separate sections within this larger unit of the grassland. There bighorn sheep and other large ungulates familiar to Lewis and Clark may sometimes be seen. These grasslands and eroded badlands also provide habitat for a wide array of other high plains mammals and birds. A checklist of 286 bird species occurring in southwestern North Dakota (including the entire region southwest of the Missouri River) has been compiled by Terry Rich. Several of these species were originally discovered by Lewis and Clark, including the greater sage-grouse, common poor-will, and McCown's longspur. Golden eagles and prairie falcons are also regular nesters here. A comparable list of 50 mammal species occurring in the same general region has been produced by Robert Seabloom and others. It includes several species that were discovered by Lewis and Clark, such as the white-tailed jackrabbit, black-tailed prairie dog, bushy-tailed woodrat, swift fox, and mule deer. Camping is permitted on both units of the national grassland.

## Lewis and Clark State Park

A park of 490 acres, located about 20 miles east of Williston off State Highway 1806, and near the Lewis and Clark campsite of April 17, 1805. Camping is permitted. The Lewis and Clark Wildlife Management Area encompasses a nearby large area of riverine lowlands and wetlands. It is located at the upper end of Lake Sakakawea and is about five miles southwest of Williston via U.S. Highway 85. There is a larger-than-life bronze statue of Sacagawea and her infant son on the state capitol grounds in Bismarck, as well as a North Dakota Heritage Center in the capitol building itself. It houses regional natural history as well as some Sacagawea lore and general expedition information.

## Fort Union Trading Post National Historic Site

This site (24 miles southwest of Williston on State Highway 1804) is located near the Lewis and Clark campsite of April 26, 1805. Fort Union (built in 1828) has been accurately recreated since 1966 on a 443-acre site, with reconstructed walls, bastions, and a trade house. The Bourgeois House serves as a museum and visitor center. This trading post was built by John J. Astor's American Fur Company in 1828, and remained active until 1867. It was 1,776 river miles from St. Louis and a major frontier fur-trading center. There is a bird checklist of 138 species. Two rather rare mixed-grass-prairie bird species, the Sprague's pipit and Baird's sparrow, were both discovered here by John J. Audubon about four decades after Lewis and Clark passed through. The Fort Union Trading Post site is near the Fort Burford State Historic Site (see below), and both were built close to the confluence of the Missouri and Yellowstone Rivers, where Fort Williams was also built in 1832. The Fort Union Trading Post was the largest in the American West, and was often visited by Native Americans representing the Crows, Crees, Blackfoot, Assiniboine, and Hunkpapa Sioux (the Lakota branch that was led into the Custer battle by Sitting Bull). It also hosted such illustrious visitors as George Catlin (1830), Karl Bodmer and Prince Maximilian (1833), and Audubon (1842).

## Fort Burford State Historic Site

Located six miles west, 14 miles southwest, and one mile south of Williston on State Highway 1804. This fort replaced the rather short-lived Fort Williams in 1866. There are only a few remnants of Fort Burford still visible, including the stone powder magazine, the Officer of the Day building, a restored field officer's quarters that is now a museum, and a military cemetery. It was to Fort Burford that Chief Joseph was brought with 400 of his Nez Percé tribe after their failed attempt to escape into Canada, and Fort Burford is also where Sitting Bull surrendered in 1881 after returning with his 187 surviving Hunkpapa Sioux followers (mostly women and children) from Canada. There is a newly constructed Confluence Area Interpretive Center at Fort Burford that deals with early exploration of the Upper Missouri region. Camping is permitted.

## Montana

## Fort Peck Indian Reservation

This enormous reservation (2,093,124 acres) was established in 1888 and is home to the Lower Assiniboine and some Sioux (Yanktonai, Oglala, and Hunkpapa) tribes. It was named for a trading post now flooded by Fort Peck Reservoir. Several annual powwows are open to the public. Located along the Lewis and Clark campsites of April 30–May 7, 1805.

## Charles M. Russell National Wildlife Refuge, Lewiston

A vast shortgrass prairie-and-badlands federal refuge, the third largest in the United States. It consists of 1,094,301 acres on both sides of Fort Peck Reservoir, once 125 river miles. It encompasses the now-impounded Lewis and Clark campsites of May 7–24, 1805. The refuge has a bird checklist of 252 species and a list of over 40 mammal species. Birds breeding here that were observed by Lewis and Clark while they were in the Great Plains include the golden eagle, greater sage-grouse, long-billed curlew, American avocet, willet, common poor-will, and black-billed magpie. Large mammals include pronghorns, mule deer, white-tailed deer, elk, and bighorns. Smaller mammals that are present and were discovered by Lewis and Clark include the black-tailed prairie dog, bushy-tailed woodrat, and white-tailed jackrabbit. There are an estimated 4,500 acres of prairie-dog towns, providing potential habitat for critically endangered black-footed ferrets, which have been released here in a restoration effort. One major access route to the western part of the refuge is possible by traveling northeast from Lewiston for 67 miles via U.S. Highway 191. Interior refuge roads are unimproved and often impassable for most vehicles. Camping is permitted. Along the mouth of the Musselshell River is the UL Bend National Wildlife Refuge (so-named for the river's meandering course there), which is continuous with the C. M. Russell NWR and is administered by it. The UL Bend NWR is even more remote than the C. M. Russell refuge. It encompasses the Lewis and Clark campsites of May 19–21, 1805.

## James Kipp State Park

This undeveloped recreation area (named after an early Indian Affairs agent who was a great friend of the northern tribes) is located off U.S. Highway 191 near the western end of C. M. Russell National Wildlife Refuge, and at the east end of the federally designated Upper Missouri National Wild and Scenic River segment. It also provides an access point for the Upper Missouri Breaks National Back Country Byway. Located near the Lewis and Clark campsite of May 24, 1805. Camping is permitted.

## Upper Missouri National Wild and Scenic River

This is a 149-mile stretch of free-flowing river, extending downstream from Fort Benton to U.S. Highway 191 and Kipp State Park. It flows through the Upper Missouri Breaks National Monument. The castlelike sandstone formations found here (the famous "White Cliffs") rise 200 to 300 feet above the river and comprise the most spectacularly beautiful part of the entire Missouri river system. They remain much as they were when Lewis and Clark saw them, and as they were painted three decades later by Karl Bodmer in 1833. They extend from near the mouth of the Marias River east for about 40 air miles or 55 river miles and are not visible by normal land access. A scenic area of similar length called the Missouri River Badlands occurs downstream. An 81-mile road loop starting and ending at Winfred is called the Missouri Breaks National Back Country Byway, but this unimproved road is suitable only for high-clearance vehicles during good weather. About nine miles west of the mouth of the Judith River, and about 1.5 miles downstream from the mouth of Arrow Creek ("Slaughter Creek" of Lewis and Clark), is the site of the buffalo jump described by Lewis and Clark, where they found more than a hundred dead bison, the animals having been stampeded by Native Americans off the brink of the steep cliffs. There is a local bird checklist of 233 species, including many of the same species that are found in the Charles M. Russell NWR. It encompasses the Lewis and Clark campsites of May 24–June 13, 1805.

## Confluence of the Marias and Missouri Rivers

At this point the expedition halted, and spent the period from June 2 to June 12 trying to establish whether the rather muddy northwestern fork or the clearer southwestern fork represented the Missouri River. Assuming that clear water meant that the southwestern stream must be coming from nearby mountains, they eventually made the proper choice and called the other stream "Maria's River," later simplified to the Marias River. They left the area in search of the Great Falls on June 12, leaving behind the larger pirogue and a cache of supplies that they planned to retrieve during the return phase. Thirteen months later, the pirogue was found to have rotted, and some of the stored materials had been flooded and destroyed, including many of the preserved plant specimens.

## Benton Lake National Wildlife Refuge, Black Eagle

A 12,383-acre marsh-and-wetland federal refuge situated 14 miles north of Great Falls. Go north from Great Falls on U.S. Highway 87 and turn left on State Highway 225 to reach the refuge entrance. The refuge's bird checklist includes 199 species and is particularly rich in wetland birds. Species breeding here that were observed by Lewis and Clark while in the Great Plains include the long-billed curlew, American avocet, willet, black-billed magpie, western meadowlark, and McCown's longspur. Nearby Fort Benton has a Wild and Scenic Upper Missouri Visitor Center and also a larger-than-life-size statue of Lewis, Clark, Sacagawea, and her son, Jean Baptiste.

## Giant Springs Heritage State Park, Great Falls

A 216-acre state park with one of the largest freshwater springs in the world. Located near the Lewis and Clark camps and portage sites of late June 1805. Nearby is Sulfur Springs, whose mineral-rich waters reputedly saved Sacagawea's life from a life-threatening illness. The Giant Springs were discovered by Captain Clark on June 18, 1805, and still produce a vast output of nearly 400 million gallons of water daily. They also represent the downstream end of the portage around Great Falls, historically a nine-mile series of five separate falls and intervening rapids, the falls representing a collective vertical height of nearly 200 feet. At the upper end of this long (18-mile) portage around the falls were several islands named the White Bear Islands by Lewis and Clark because of the numerous grizzly bears they found there. During the outward-bound phase of the expedition, 11 days (June 21 to July 2, 1804) were needed for the overland route; on the return phase only eight days were needed, as horses were then available for hauling. Also located at the state park is the Lewis and Clark National Historic Trail Interpretive Center, operated by the U.S. Forest Service and home to the Lewis and Clark Trail Heritage Foundation.

## Ulm Piskun State Park

A 170-acre state park with a mile-long "piskun," a place where bison were stampeded into confined corrals or forced to jump from steep cliffs. This is probably the largest reported such site in the United States, and has a 30-foot cliff-face. A captive bison herd is present. Located about five miles west of the Great Falls airport and in the general vicinity of the Lewis and Clark campsites of July 10–14, 1805.

## Holter Lake and Sleeping Giant Special Recreation Areas, Wolf Creek

Includes a reservoir (Holter Lake) surrounded by the Gates of the Mountains Wilderness and Beartooth State Game Range. The entire area collectively covers about 18,000 acres. Captain Lewis gave this part of the river its present evocative name, "Gates of the Rocky Mountains." Located near the Lewis and Clark campsites of July 18–20, 1805. Holter Dam has raised the river's water level about 100 feet and is one of three dams in the region (the others are Hauser and Canyon Ferry) that have collectively produced a nearly continuous 70-mile impoundment. Nearby, along Prickly Pear Creek, is where Lewis first briefly observed Lewis's woodpecker, which he later (May 27, 1806) described in detail from a specimen shot in Idaho. Camping is permitted.

## Canyon Ferry State Park and State Wildlife Management Area

A 3,500-acre state park and wildlife area surrounding Canyon Ferry Reservoir. Located along the Lewis and Clark campsites of July 20–27, 1805. Camping is permitted in the state park.

## Missouri Headwaters State Park, Three Forks

A 527-acre state park at the confluence of the Gallatin, Madison, and Jefferson Rivers. Located near the Lewis and Clark campsite of July 27–30, 1805. The site was first recognized by Lewis and Clark as representing the primary origin of the Missouri River, although the actual snowmelt headwaters derive from many small sources high in the mountains. Captain Clark and his group were the first members of the expedition to arrive at the headwaters on July 25 and were followed by the rest of the group on July 27. The entire expedition remained there until July 30, when they began the ascent up the Jefferson and Beaverhead Rivers, followed by challenging the Rocky Mountains themselves. The same campsite was used by Captain Clark and his contingent during the return trip on July 13, 1806. The state park has interpretive exhibits with information on Lewis and Clark. Camping is permitted. Also near Three Forks is Madison Buffalo Jump State Park.

## Pompeys Pillar National Monument

Located near the Yellowstone River, 28 miles east of Billings, and off Exit 23 from I-94. This 200-foot sandstone promontory was named "Pompy's Tower" by Captain Clark after Sacagawea's son, Jean Baptiste ("Pompy") Charbonneau, then about 18 months old. Clark's dated, carved signature is still visible in the soft rock. Located between the Clark campsites of July 25 and 26, 1806. Nearby is the Pompey's Pillar Visitor Center.

# References

Bailey, V. 1928. *A Biological Survey of North Dakota.* North American Fauna, no. 49. Washington DC: Bureau of Biological Survey.

Barkley, T. M., ed. 1977. *Atlas of the Flora of the Great Plains.* Ames: Iowa Sate University Press.

―――. 1986. *Flora of the Great Plains.* Lawrence: University Press of Kansas.

Biddle, N., ed. 1814. *History of the Expedition under the Commands of Captains Lewis and Clark to the Sources of the Missouri, etc. During the years 1804–5–6.* 2 vols. Philadelphia: Paul Allen. Reprinted in 3 vols., 1815.

Brown, C. J. D. 1971. *Fishes of Montana.* Bozeman MT: Big Sky Books.

Brown, J. E. 1992. *Animals of the Soul: Sacred Animals of the Oglala Sioux.* Rockport MA: Element Press.

Burroughs, R. D. 1961. *The Natural History of the Lewis and Clark Expedition.* East Lansing: Michigan State University Press.

―――. 1966. The Lewis and Clark Expedition's botanical discoveries. *Natural History* 75 (1): 56–62.

Cahalane, V. H., ed. 1967. *The Imperial Collection of Audubon Mammals: The Quadrupeds of North America.* New York: Bonanza Books.

Clark, T. W., and M. R. Stromberg. 1987. *Mammals in Wyoming.* Public Education ser. no. 10. Lawrence: University of Kansas Museum of Natural History.

Coues, E. 1876. An account of the various publications relating to the travels of Lewis and Clark, with a commentary on the zoological results of their expedition. *Bulletin of the U.S. Geological and Geographical Surveys of the Territories,* no. 6, 2d ser., pp. 417–44. Washington DC: Government Printing Office.

―――. [1893] 1965. *History of the Expedition under the Command of Lewis and Clark.* 3 vols. Reprint, New York: Dover Publications. Meteorological Register is in vol. 3, pp. 1264–98.

―――. 1898. Notes on Mr. Thomas Meehan's paper on the plants of Lewis' and Clark's expedition across the continent. *Proceedings of the Academy of Natural Sciences of Philadelphia* 50:291–315.

Cutright, P. R. 1968. Meriwether Lewis: botanist. *Oregon Historical Quarterly* 69:148–70.

———. [1969] 1989. *Lewis and Clark: Pioneering Naturalists.* Reprint, Lincoln: University of Nebraska Press.

———. 1984. A history of Lewis's woodpecker and Clark's nutcracker. *We Proceeded On* (Lewis and Clark Trail Heritage Foundation) 10 (2–3): 9–15.

Ducey, J. E. 1988. *Nebraska Birds: Breeding Status and Distribution.* Omaha: Simmons-Boardman Books.

———. 2000. *Birds of the Untamed West: The History of Birdlife in Nebraska, 1750–1875.* Omaha: Making History Press.

Faxon, W. 1915. Relics of Peale's Museum. *Bulletin of the Museum of Comparative Zoology* 59:119–48. Mentions the only known original Lewis's woodpecker specimen.

Ferris, R. G. 1975. *Lewis and Clark: Historic Places Associated with their Transcontinental Exploration (1804–06).* National Survey of Historic Sites and Buildings, vol. 12. Washington DC: U.S. Department of the Interior.

Finch, D. M. 1992. Threatened, endangered and vulnerable species of terrestrial vertebrates in the Rocky Mountain region. Gen. Tech. Rept. RM-215. Fort Collins CO: USDA Forest Service, Rocky Mountain Forest and Range Experiment Station.

Forsman, K. R. 2001. *The Wild Mammals of Montana.* Lawrence KS: American Society of Mammalogists.

Geist, V. 1996. *Buffalo Nation: History and Legends of the North American Bison.* Stillwater MN: Voyageur Press.

Gilmore, M. R. [1919] 1977. *Uses of Plants by the Indians of the Upper Missouri River Region.* Reprint, Lincoln: University of Nebraska Press. Originally published as *Thirty-third Annual Report of the Bureau of American Ethnology,* Washington DC.

Higgins, K. F., E. D. Stukel, J. M. Goulet, and D. C. Backlund. 2000. *Wild Mammals of South Dakota.* Pierre: South Dakota Department of Game, Fish and Parks.

Hoberg, T., and C. Gause. 1992. Reptiles and amphibians of North Dakota. *North Dakota Outdoors* 55 (1): 7–19. Also available online at the Northern Prairie Wildlife Research Center's website, *http://www.npwrc.usgs.gov/resource/distr/herps/amrepnd/amrepnd.htm* (Version 16JUL97).

Hoffman, R. S., and D. L. Pattie. 1968. *A Guide to Montana Mammals.* Missoula: University of Montana Press.

Holmgren, V. C. 1984. Birds of the Lewis and Clark journals. *We Proceeded On* (Lewis and Clark Trail Heritage Foundation) 10 (2–3): 17–22.

———. 1984. A glossary of bird names cited by Lewis and Clark. *We Proceeded On* (Lewis and Clark Trail Heritage Foundation) 10 (2–3): 28–34.

————. 1984. Summary of birds seen by Lewis and Clark. *We Proceeded On* (Lewis and Clark Trail Heritage Foundation) 10 (2–3): 23–26.

Jensen, B. 2001. Lewis and Clark in North Dakota: Wildlife then and now—A brief natural history of North Dakota, 1804 to present. *North Dakota Outdoors* 63 (9): 10–19. Also available online at the Northern Prairie Wildlife Research Center's website, *http://www.npwrc.usgs.gov/resource/2001/thennow/thennow. htm* (Version 13NOV2001).

Johnsgard, P. A. 1979. *Birds of the Great Plains: Breeding Species and Their Distribution.* Lincoln: University of Nebraska Press.

————. 2001. *The Nature of Nebraska: Ecology and Biodiversity.* Lincoln: University of Nebraska Press.

Jones, J. K., D. M. Armstrong, and J. R. Choate. 1985. *Guide to Mammals of the Plains States.* Lincoln: University of Nebraska Press.

Jones, J. K., D. M. Armstrong, R. S. Hoffmann, and C. Jones. 1983. *Mammals of the Northern Great Plains.* Lincoln: University of Nebraska Press.

Kindscher, K. 1987. *Edible Wild Plants of the Prairie: An Ethnobotanical Guide.* Lawrence: University Press of Kansas.

————. 1992. *Medicinal Wild Plants of the Prairie.* Lawrence: University Press of Kansas.

Meehan, T. 1898. The plants of Lewis' and Clark's expedition across the continent. *Proceedings of the Academy of Natural Sciences of Philadelphia* 50:12–49.

Moulton, G. E., ed. 1983–2001. *The Journals of the Lewis and Clark Expedition.* 13 vols. Lincoln: University of Nebraska Press.

Mutel, C. F. 1989. *Fragile Giants: A Natural History of the Loess Hills.* Iowa City: University of Iowa Press.

Nelson, R. A. 1979. *Handbook of Rocky Mountain Plants.* 3d ed. Estes Park CO: Skyland Publishers.

Phillips, H. Wayne. 2003. *Plants of the Lewis and Clark Expedition.* Missoula: Mountain Press.

Plamondon, M. II. 2000, 2002. *Lewis and Clark Trail Maps: A Cartographic Reconstruction.* 2 vols. Pullman: Washington State University Press.

Reid, R., and C. G. Gannon. 1999. Birds and mammals observed by Lewis and Clark in North Dakota. *North Dakota History* 66 (2): 2–14.

Reveal, J. L., G. E. Moulton, and A. E. Schuyler. 1999. The Lewis and Clark collections of vascular plants: Names, types and comments. *Publications of the Academy of Natural Sciences of Philadelphia* 149:1–64.

Rich, T. 1992. Birds of southwestern North Dakota. Bureau of Land Management, Dickinson ND. Unpaginated. Also available online at the Northern Prairie Wildlife Research Center's website, *http://www.npwrc.usgs.gov/resource/2001/ thennow/thennow.htm.*

Ronda, J. P. 1984, *Lewis and Clark among the Indians.* Lincoln: University of Nebraska Press.

Rudd, V. E. 1954. Botanical contributions of the Lewis and Clark Expedition. *Journal of the Washington Academy of Sciences* 44:351–56.

Seabloom, R. W., R. D. Crawford, and M. G. McKenna. 1978. *Vertebrates of Southwestern North Dakota: Amphibians, Reptiles, Birds, Mammals.* Grand Forks ND: Institute for Ecological Studies, University of North Dakota. Also available online at the Northern Prairie Wildlife Research Center's website, *http://www.npwrc.usgs.gov/resource/2001/thennow/thennow.htm.*

Schmidt, T. 2002. *Guide to the Lewis and Clark Trail.* Washington DC: National Geographic Society.

Setzer, H. W. 1954. Zoological contributions of the Lewis and Clark Expedition. *Journal of the Washington Academy of Sciences* 44:356–57.

Sharpe, R. S., W. R. Silcock, and J. G. Jorgensen. 2001. *Birds of Nebraska: Their Distribution and Temporal Occurrence.* Lincoln: University of Nebraska Press.

South Dakota Ornithologists' Union (SDOU). 1991. *The Birds of South Dakota.* 2d ed. Aberdeen SD: SDOU.

Stevens, O. A. 1950. *Handbook of North Dakota Plants.* Fargo: North Dakota Institute for Regional Studies.

Stewart, R. E. 1975. *Breeding Birds of North Dakota.* Fargo: Tri-College Center for Environmental Studies.

Swenk, M. H. 1935. A history of Nebraska ornithology, III: Period of the explorations of the early nineteenth century. The Lewis and Clark and Zebulon M. Pike expeditions. *Nebraska Bird Review* 3:115–24.

Thompson, M. C., and C. Ely. 1989, 1992. *Birds in Kansas.* 2 vols. Lawrence: University Press of Kansas.

Thwaites, R. G., ed. 1904–5. *Original Journals of the Lewis and Clark Expedition, 1804–1806.* 7 vols., atlas. New York: Dodd, Mead and Co.

Todd, K. 2002. *What's Lost, What's Left: A Status Report on the Plants and Animals of the Lewis and Clark Expedition.* Seattle: Sierra Club. Online version available at: *sierraclub.org/lewisandclark.*

U.S. Fish and Wildlife Service. 1995. North Dakota's federally listed endangered, threatened, and candidate species. Bismarck ND: U.S. Fish and Wildlife Service. Available online at the Northern Prairie Wildlife Research Center's website, *http://www.npwrc.usgs.gov/resource/distr/others/nddanger/nddanger. htm* (Version 16JUL97).

Van Bruggen, T. 1985. *The Vascular Plants of South Dakota.* 2d ed. Ames: Iowa State University Press.

Walcheck, K. C. 1969. Birds observed by Lewis and Clark in Montana, 1805–1806. *Proceedings of the Montana Academy of Sciences* 29:13–29.

————. 1976. Montana wildlife 170 years ago. *Montana Outdoors* 7 (4): 15–30.

————. 1976. Lewis and Clark meet the awesome white bear. *Montana Outdoors* 7(5):42–45.

Webb, W. P. 1931. *The Great Plains.* New York: Grosset and Dunlap.

Wilson, A. 1808–14. *American Ornithology.* 9 vols. Philadelphia: Bradford and Inskeep.

Winkler, S. 1990. *The Smithsonian Guide to Historic America: The Plains States.* New York: Steward, Tabori and Chang.

# Index to Places, Plants, and Animals

Plants and animals are indexed under the English and Latin names preferentially used in the text. Alternate English names have been excluded. Illustrations are indicated by italics. Counties, cities, and other present-day political units are not indexed.